ON FRIENDSHIP

Matteo Ricci and Xu Guangqi, from Athanasius Kircher,
China Illustrata (1667). (Collection of the translator)

ON FRIENDSHIP

One Hundred Maxims for a Chinese Prince

交友論

MATTEO RICCI

Translated by
TIMOTHY BILLINGS

COLUMBIA UNIVERSITY PRESS / *New York*

Columbia University Press
Publishers Since 1893
New York   Chichester, West Sussex
Copyright © 2009 Columbia University Press

Library of Congress Cataloging-in-Publication Data
Ricci, Matteo, 1552–1610.
[Jiaoyou lun. English]
On friendship : one hundred maxims for a Chinese prince /
Matteo Ricci ; translated by Timothy Billings.
p. cm.
Includes bibliographical references and index.
ISBN 978-0-231-14924-2 (cloth : alk. paper) ISBN 978-0-231-52028-7 (e-book)
1. Friendship—Quotations, maxims, etc. 2. Conduct of life—Quotations,
maxims, etc. I. Billings, Timothy James, 1963– II. Title.
BJ1533.F8R4913 2009
177'.62—dc22
2009019567

Columbia University Press books are printed on
permanent and durable acid-free paper.
This book is printed on paper with recycled content.
Printed in the United States of America

c 10 9 8 7 6 5 4 3 2

For

Natasha V. Chang

我之半

and

Haun Saussy

知己之友

Contents

ix   *Acknowledgments*

1   INTRODUCTION

84   交友論 / ON FRIENDSHIP

139   *Chronology of Editions*

143   *Texts and Variants*

157   *Sources and Notes*

167   *Index*

A C K N O W L E D G M E N T S

Anyone who has ever written a book knows what it means to rely on friends of many qualities and degrees for support, but it is rare to write a book that forces one constantly to reflect on the nature of the friendships that have enabled one to write a book. I have felt the temptation to thank absolutely everyone whom I have ever regarded with the slightest hint of amical affection and to boast myself rich in the possession of so many "friends," both illustrious and little known. But I am persuaded to allow my friends both distant and close to recognize themselves in the pages herein, and to content myself with naming only those who have contributed materially to the production of this book. Foremost among them is Jennifer Crewe, the best friend a scholar could hope to have. Without her sponsorship, this book might never have seen print. For reading drafts at various stages and contributing invaluable criticism, I am indebted to Andrew Lo and Haun Saussy, as well as to David Mungello and Thierry Meynard. They have honored this book with their attention, and it is so much the better for their comments. Thanks also to Yan Zinan for his willingness to puzzle out difficult passages with a ready laugh, to Zhang Kai for helping me resolve the last grammatical puzzle, to Chen Liyuan for the early support that launched this project, to Emily Asher for drafting the index, and to Mike Ashby for his meticulous and informed copyediting. I would also like to thank the American Academy in Rome, where I drafted a portion of this translation, especially Pina Pasquantonio, for making my visit there so comfortable. I owe a debt of gratitude to the staff in the manuscripts departments of the British Library, the Bibliothèque nationale de France, the Biblioteca Apostolica Vaticana, and the Biblioteca nazionale centrale, but most of all to the exceptionally warm and helpful staff at the library of the Institut des Hautes Études Chinoises, at the Collège de France, Paris, whom I shall dare to call my friends. I owe a debt to Middlebury College not only for giving me a home with many friends but also for allowing me to leave it, as well as for a subvention that supported the publication of this book. Most of all, I cannot sufficiently express my gratitude to the board of the Andrew W. Mellon Foundation for the extremely generous New Directions Fellowship, which made research for this book and other incipient projects possible—especially to Joseph Miesel, who facilitated every stage of my research and travel with alacrity.

Most people should not embark casually upon writing a book, because a book claims a portion of one's life and changes it. For my part, I did not elect this book casually, but rather decided deliberately one day to write it in order to have something worthy of Haun Saussy, whose friendship has buoyed me as I imagine the great friendships of antiquity once comforted and nourished those more eminent than I could ever hope to be. I cannot help but feel that the product falls short of that worthiness, but I know that he will accept it nevertheless—just as he will accept that I cannot dedicate it solely to him because of that other, singular friend who rejoices and suffers with me daily, and who has done so daily as I labored to bring this book to completion. The ancients would no doubt be disappointed with me for making the classic mistake of confusing love with friendship, but I am certain that Natasha Chang is not just the love of my life but also the best friend that I have ever known, my other half, my other self. If Haun was the reason I started this book, Natasha is the reason I finished it. And so it is to them both that I dedicate it.

On Friendship

INTRODUCTION

I n 1595, when an upstart player named William Shakespeare was writing a fantastical comedy in English verse called *A Midsummer Night's Dream* for the London stage, on the opposite side of the globe, in the southern Chinese city of Nanchang 南昌, an equally remarkable man named Matteo Ricci was composing an essay on friendship in the formal diction of classical Chinese. Ricci called his essay simply *You lun* 友論 (*Essay on Friends*), a title that would later be changed under the influence of one of Ricci's many Chinese friends to the more resonant *Jiaoyou lun* 交友論 (*Essay on Friendship*), the name by which it is known and loved by Chinese intellectuals even today.

For many readers, Matteo Ricci needs no introduction. To anyone with a high-school education in China, he is also instantly recognizable by the Chinese name that he chose for himself, Li Madou 利瑪竇. As a talented scholar with an extraordinary memory and a gift for languages, as the most eminent cofounder of the Jesuit mission in China (which Saint Francis Xavier had struggled in vain to establish shortly before his death off the coast of China in 1552), as the first European to gain access to the imperial Forbidden City in Beijing, and as the first European to have his writings included in an imperial anthology (including this essay on friendship), Ricci has become almost legendary as a figure who braved apparently insurmountable odds in order to forge meaningful cultural connections between Europe and China. Even as a Christian missionary whose chief aim was the saving of souls through baptism and conversion, Ricci has been admired — and also severely criticized — for his attempts to adapt or "accommodate" Christian teachings to Chinese cultural expectations in addition to spreading secular European knowledge related to cartography, mathematics, astronomy, mechanics, philosophy, music, and visual art. After a dozen tumultuous years in southern China, Ricci was still five years away from obtaining permission to visit the imperial court in Beijing at the time that he wrote this essay on friendship, but his intelligence and his familiarity with the Confucian classics along with his dignified bearing had already begun to earn him influential Chinese friends of the scholar-official class. The essay would win him many more.

In fact, the staggering popularity of the essay was to play a crucial role in all his subsequent missionary efforts by establishing Ricci's reputation as a Western sage whose unusual teachings were worthy of consideration. Within a year of its composition, Ricci wrote in a letter to Rome: "There are so many people who ask to see it and to transcribe it that I never have any copies on hand to show."[1] The same year, in 1596, a local official from a nearby town who had become a great friend to the Jesuits decided to have it published without Ricci's knowledge.[2] (Ricci stressed this point, since the Jesuits were not allowed to print without approval from Rome, which could take years, but in the same letter he also praised the friend's good soul for doing so.) Within the next five years, two other editions were independently printed, in 1599 and 1601, by two other Chinese friends, also without Ricci's permission or knowledge, thus quickly turning it into the late Ming equivalent of a best seller. In a letter of

1599, Ricci wrote: "This *Friendship* has earned more credit for me and for our Europe than anything else that we have done; because the others do us credit for mechanical and artificial things of hands and tools; but this does us credit for literature, for wit, and for virtue."[3] A decade later, in 1609, when Ricci was compiling his journals for later publication in Europe, he reported that the essay still "astounds all the kingdom" (fa stupire a tutto questo regno), that it had been repeatedly printed both in Beijing and in other provinces with great applause from all scholars, that it had made for him many friendships and caused him to be known by many important people, and that it had already begun to be quoted in important Chinese books.[4]

Ricci probably knew that as early as 1602 about a third of the essay had been excerpted with slight revisions to the style in Wang Kentang's 王肯堂 (1549–1613) influential anthology *Yugang zhai bizhu* 鬱剛齋筆麈 (*Pen Notes from the Lush Ridge Studio*).[5] But the extraordinary popularity of the work is demonstrated by its repeated anthologizing in full or in part by other Chinese writers after Ricci's death, including such authors as Wu Congxian 吳從先 (1614), Chen Jiru 陳繼儒 (1615), Jiang Xuqi 江旭奇 (1616), Feng Kebin 馮可賓 (1622), Zhu Tingdan 朱廷但 (1626), and Tao Zongyi 陶宗儀 (1646).[6] In addition to all these versions, Ricci's friend and former collaborator, Li Zhizao 李之藻 (1565–1630), prepared what has long been considered to be the definitive edition (although it bears some of the latter's emendations) in a multivolume anthology of Jesuit Chinese writings printed two decades after Ricci's death as the *Tianxue chuhan* 天學初函 (*First Writings of Heavenly Studies*, 1629).[7]

Most impressively of all, the whole of Ricci's work (lacking only the proem) was reprinted in the first of the great imperial libraries, or *congshu*

叢書 (collectanea), of the eighteenth century, the *Gujin tushu jicheng* 古今圖書集成 (*The Compendium of Ancient and Modern Books and Illustrations*, hereafter *TSJC*) in 1725. Ricci had written brief commentaries to a number of maxims using the half-size characters normally reserved for scholarly exegesis on classical texts, thus cleverly creating for his text the look and feel of an instant classic. At the end of the essay, however, the editors of the *TSJC* write: "Note: Since the *Essay on Friends* is literature from the Western Regions, the explanatory comments are extremely difficult to understand!" (按友論乃西域文注辭多費解). To be sure, the commentaries rarely do more than repeat the main idea of the maxim, but a couple of them are genuinely original attempts at cultural synthesis. Yet just as interesting as the inclusion of the essay in the *TSJC* is the essay's exclusion, half a century later, in 1773, from the even larger imperial collectanea, the *Siku quanshu* 四庫全書 (*Complete Writings of the Four Treasuries*, hereafter *SKQS*), perhaps because of a shift in attitudes toward the Jesuits, or perhaps because discourses on "friendship" were increasingly criticized as covert expressions of anti-Manchu factionalism.

Ricci's work also seems to have become standard reading for subsequent Jesuit missionaries in China, probably as a classical language primer; and its continued popularity seems to have been the motivation, some fifty years later, in 1647, for another gifted Italian Jesuit, Martino Martini, to write a sequel to it: *Qiuyou pian* 逑友篇 (*Pamphlet on Gathering Friends*). The fact that Martini's treatise is several times longer, heavily didactic, and much more explicitly religious in content may partly account for why it has been almost completely forgotten, in contrast to the enduring success of Ricci's original.

Considering its unique status as the first work by a European to be included in Chinese collectanea, Ricci's essay has been strangely neglected by non-Chinese scholars, partly perhaps because its central theme of friendship has attracted less interest among missionary and intellectual historians than the theological and philosophical content of Ricci's later Chinese masterwork, the *Tianzhu shiyi* 天主實義 (*The True Meaning of the Lord in Heaven*, 1603). Indeed, the essay is so little known in non-Chinese scholarship that it is often incorrectly described in studies of Ricci's life and work as a dialogue in imitation of Cicero's famous treatise on friendship from the first century B.C.E. In recent years, however, cultural historians have begun to recognize how important friendship was as a topic of great interest to late Ming intellectuals, who wrote about it almost obsessively, which suggests that Ricci was attempting to participate in, and to benefit from, a discussion that was already taking place in China.

BACKGROUND AND COMPOSITION

Born on October 6, 1552, just a couple of months before Saint Francis Xavier's death, Matteo Ricci grew up in Macerata, an important provincial center in central-eastern Italy and one of the Papal States; attended the newly established Jesuit school there in his youth; and then initially studied law at La Sapienza, in Rome, at the insistence of his father before choosing to pursue the study of theology and mathematics at the Jesuit colleges in Rome and Coimbra, Portugal. He departed from Lisbon in 1578 for the four-and-a-half-month journey to the mission in

Goa, where he continued his studies for the next few years, except for a brief period in 1580 in Kochi (Cochin), in southwestern India, where he was ordained. Two years later, Ricci was sent to the Portuguese-Chinese port city of Macao to begin learning Chinese. After less than a year, in September 1583, Ricci entered China proper in the company of Michele Ruggieri (1543–1607), another Italian Jesuit several years Ricci's senior who had begun to study Chinese a few years earlier. Ruggieri had made a few unsuccessful forays into the Chinese mainland before he finally managed to secure permission from the governor of the city of Zhaoqing 肇慶, in the southern province of Guangdong 廣東, to establish a house that would be the Jesuits' first foothold in the ancient kingdom.

It is humbling to consider that before entering China in 1583, Ricci had spent less than a year studying Chinese, without any of the aids now considered essential to modern language students—bilingual dictionaries, pronunciation CDs, workbooks, and the occasional video—but in the intervening dozen years before he first drafted his essay on friendship, Ricci's knowledge of the language had increased to a level that any student would envy; and he did it while struggling along with a handful of fellow Jesuits to establish a stable mission in southern China amid mistrust, suspicion, and mild persecution from the local residents. This is not the place to recount those stories, but it should be noted that only five years after arriving in Zhaoqing, Ruggieri returned, in 1588, to Italy and never went back to China—an enormous loss to the mission—and the following year, Ricci and his confreres were evicted from their newly built house, which was seized by a new viceroy, who offered them a token payment in compensation (which Ricci refused). The sensible Chinese laws directed at controlling corruption and favoritism by transferring local officials to new posts every few years unfortunately proved to be a challenge to the Jesuits, who found that their permission to keep residence was as impermanent as the appointment of the official who granted it, especially in a climate of general distrust toward foreigners.

After a difficult period of uncertainty, Ricci finally secured, the following year, an invitation to resettle in Shaozhou 韶州, a city slightly to the north of Zhaoqing, thus beginning another brief residence marked by cultural and missionary successes as well as trials in the form of harassment from neighbors. Then, in 1595, Ricci ambitiously made his first attempt to reach the imperial court in Beijing, traveling northward through Nanchang (the capital of Jiangxi 江西 Province) to the former southern imperial capital, Nanjing 南京. But as fate and the Chinese bureaucracy would have it, Ricci was refused permission to travel any farther northward and even to remain in Nanjing, which forced him to retrace his steps to Nanchang, where—as he recounts in his proem to the essay—he decided to stay.

A Princely Gift

In Nanchang, Ricci attracted the attention of Jian'an Wang 建安王 (the Prince of Jian'an Commandery), a distant cousin of the emperor, to whom Ricci presented his essay on friendship as a gift.[8] From the description in Ricci's proem, it seems that, after the prince had banqueted Ricci one evening at his estate, the conversation turned to the topic of friendship— as it was likely to do among male intellectuals in this period—and the prince seems to have expressed a desire to know more about what Europeans thought about the topic. According to Ricci's proem, he then went home, gathered everything that he could remember from his youthful studies of classical literature about friendship, and wrote the essay for the prince. We now know that Ricci seems to have jogged his memory about those youthful studies with the help of a sixteenth-century Latin "commonplace book" (a sort of Renaissance Bartlett's *Familiar Quotations*), *Sententiae et exempla* (*Wise Sayings and Illustrative Anecdotes*), compiled by the Portuguese scholar Andrea de Rèsende (1498–1573)—or Andreas Eborensis, as he is known in Latin—the fifth edition of which was published in 1590, just in time to be sent to China for Ricci to use.[9] It would be too cynical to doubt the veracity of Ricci's anecdote altogether, since Ricci's journals confirm that he visited the prince on multiple occasions, presented him with a number of gifts, and received from him many favors. It seems clear that, by almost any definition, they were friends. And yet there is more to the story.

One year after the composition of the essay, in a letter to the Jesuit superior Claudio Aquaviva in Rome (Nanchang, October 13, 1596), Ricci writes: "Last year, as an exercise, I wrote in Chinese several sayings *On Friendship*, selected from the best of our books; and since they were from so varied and eminent personages, the literati of this land were left astonished, and, in order to give it more authority, I wrote an introduction and gave it as a present to a certain relative of the king's, who also has the title of king."[10] The essay thus evidently began as a mere translation exercise, which was much admired by the Chinese scholars to whom he showed it; only afterward did Ricci add the proem, with its anecdote about Jian'an Wang, "in order to give it more authority." Three years later, in a letter to Girolamo Costa, in Rome (Nanjing, August 15, 1599), Ricci writes:

And because Y[our] R[everence] asked me for several things from here, I will send you enclosed herein certain sayings about friends that I wrote four years ago now in the province of Jiangxi at the request of a relative of the king's, who lived there, who has the title and state of a king but without his own kingdom, and together with this I will send you the translation in Italian; but it cannot have the grace of the Chinese language, because I accommodated myself in every way to them, and, where it was necessary, I changed several things in the sayings and sententiae of our philosophers, [and] some things I took from our Christian writers.[11]

Ricci's tale thus gradually evolved as he decided to promote the literary fiction recorded in the proem itself rather than the less appealing story about recycling a composition exercise. (Note that Ricci says he "accommodated" himself, and that he is sending a "translation in Italian"— points to which I return in the next two sections.)

Nevertheless, Ricci certainly presented his essay as a gift, even if he did not begin writing it as a gift. In 1609, a year before his death, Ricci set about redrafting the diaries, mission records, and memories of nearly three decades in China into a formal narrative in Italian that he clearly intended for publication, the most obvious sign of which is that he constantly refers to himself in the third person. In these "journals," Ricci reports that the essay was one of two books that he presented to the prince, which pleased him more than any of his other gifts—the first of which was an illustrated description of the world, the nine celestial spheres, and various mathematical demonstrations: "The other was a treatise *On Friendship*, in which, pretending [*fingendo*] that the same King asked the

Father [Ricci] what they had heard in Europe about friendship in the form of a dialogue, the Father furthermore answered him with everything that he was able to gather together from our philosophers, saints, and all authors old and new. And he made a work that even now astonishes the whole kingdom."[12] In that *fingendo*, Ricci openly acknowledges the innocent literary pretense of having invented a brief conversation in his proem in which the prince requests such a work on friendship, which is consistent with the story in his first letter—and the prince seems to have been delighted by it.[13]

Uncomfortable Accommodations

When Ricci sat down to compose the essay, even after a dozen years of intensive language study, he was still relatively new to writing in Chinese. With the exception of a collaboration with Ruggieri on a Chinese catechism and perhaps also an abandoned early draft of the opening of Euclid's *Elements* (which would be completed years later with the help of the high-ranking convert Xu Guangqi 徐光啟 [1592–1633]), Ricci's only other formal writing in Chinese had been the long captions on a wall-size world map. (According to his journals, however, Ricci himself considered the essay to be his first work in Chinese.)[14] Hung on the wall of the Jesuit house for all guests to see, this *mappamondo* astonished Chinese visitors both because it provocatively suggested that China was not exactly at the center of the world and because it included so many countries and place-names far beyond the confines of China that nobody had ever heard of before. For the first time, they were introduced to such exotic-sounding places as Luoma 羅馬 (Roma), where there lived the leader of a religion followed by all the countries in the West; a peaceful island called Ai-er-lan 愛爾蘭 (Ireland), which had no poisonous snakes or toads; as well as a huge landmass at the southern pole where very large parrots were said to live.[15] As a corrective to the typical story of how the Jesuits brought Western science, mathematics, astronomy, and cartography to the "unenlightened" Chinese people, it is helpful to be reminded on occasion that, as men of the seventeenth century, the Jesuits had certain limitations of their own, from anatomy to astronomy, including not least of all a papal injunction to adhere to a geocentric cosmology (which some quietly disobeyed).[16]

Ricci created multiple versions of the famous *mappamondo* and eventually had it published. Years later, the emperor would request a personal copy of the wall-size version, which Ricci made himself.

Thus it is notable that the first two Chinese works that Ricci undertook were essentially secular: Ricci mentions "God" in only two of the one hundred maxims on friendship (maxims 16 and 56). One prominent historian of the China mission, David Mungello, sees these choices as strategic: "The choice of the accommodative theme of friendship by Martini, and before him by Ricci, signifies one path which the Jesuits cultivated to Chinese literati souls."[17] In other words, Ricci's essay was an early implementation of the controversial Jesuit strategy of accommodation—that is, the adaptation of the practices and teachings of Christianity as much as possible to local cultures without losing the essence of the doctrine. Accommodation also took the more mundane form of adopting the dress, etiquette, and, of course, language of a local culture in order to proselytize more effectively. It should be noted that the debates over missionary accommodation, especially in China, extended a century beyond Ricci's lifetime, and that within years of his death they would explode into the so-called Rites Controversy. The issue at stake was whether the universal Confucian rites of paying respects to images of family ancestors and even to Confucius himself were a form of pagan worship, and therefore to be banned from practice among Christian converts, or whether they were simply a secular expression of respect to one's forebears and philosophical teachers and therefore to be allowed. Late in life, Ricci seems to have come around to acknowledging that they were truly a form of worship, which would have immensely complicated the Jesuits' proselytizing efforts, but his fellow Jesuits posthumously suppressed Ricci's comments on the subject. In the end, the pope finally decided against "ancestor worship," which dealt a severe blow to the Jesuit China mission.[18]

In 1595, however, Ricci was still looking for new accommodative methods. Thus one way of understanding the motivation of Ricci's essay on friendship is as an effort to accommodate in the broadest sense — to establish a common ground for cross-cultural understanding, respect, and goodwill; or, as we might also say, to make friends — in order to pave the way for proselytizing. And even if this view seems to underestimate the potential personal interest that Ricci may have taken in wanting to make Chinese friends for the sake of genuine friendship, it would be naive to think that he did not have the ultimate goal of converting souls in mind when writing it.

It would also be misleading to imagine that Ricci wrote the essay absolutely and entirely by himself, since the Jesuits always had the assistance of hired native Chinese tutors in polishing the style of their prose, in addition to help from one another. Considering that Ricci seems to have begun the essay as a translation exercise on a popular topic, its composition would seem to differ from Ricci's later collaborations with Xu Guangqi and Li Zhizao in translating extremely technical works of mathematics and astronomy, in which the labors of interpreting, translating, and composing were probably more evenly divided. But it is important to stress that almost everything the Jesuits did was collective and that many of the Chinese scholars who quoted or printed Ricci's maxims revised them, even if only slightly, in a further stage of collaboration. These ideas are helpful to bear in mind as a corrective to the familiar notion of the unique genius working in isolation (which is no more true of Ricci than of Shakespeare). And we should consider the very existence of those early Chinese translations of European scientific works to be a testimony to cross-cultural friendship itself, since without it, they could never have been done.[19]

TWO MANUSCRIPTS, TWO MATTEOS

One of the long-standing mysteries about the essay on friendship is a puzzling manuscript apparently dating to the late sixteenth century: it contains a loose Italian translation that is strangely oblique and sometimes slightly inaccurate of only seventy-six of the full one hundred maxims, all written in a single unidentified hand that is certainly not Ricci's. Now conserved in the archives of the Pontificia Università Gregoriana (hereafter PUG), this manuscript was long and incorrectly assumed to be the missing enclosure mentioned by Ricci in his letter (August 15, 1599) to Girolamo Costa. For lack of a better explanation, the translation was published in Italy in 1825 as Ricci's own.

At the turn of the new millennium, however, during a project at the British Library (hereafter BL) to catalog and photograph the rare manuscripts formerly owned by Frederick North, the fifth Earl of Guilford (1791–1827), a manuscript was discovered in North's collection that appears to be the missing manuscript that Ricci had originally enclosed in his letter. It was acquired by the library in the early nineteenth century, but somehow it had never come to the attention of Ricci scholars before the Guilford project. The BL manuscript is written in Ricci's own distinctive hand, and it includes both the Chinese text and Ricci's own Italian translation (a more accurate version than that in the anonymous PUG manuscript), along with romanized pronunciations alongside every character. The Italian sinologist Filippo Mignini, the first to study the new text, argues that the newly discovered BL manuscript was the direct source for the strange translation in the PUG manuscript, and that the latter translation was an attempt by someone in Italy to adapt the style and content of Ricci's translation to make it less "Chinese" and more palatable to Christian European readers.[20] In fact, a close comparison of the BL manuscript with the original Chinese text shows that Ricci had already made certain concessions to European or Christian ideas in his *own* Italian translation there, so the paraphrastic PUG manuscript actually represents an adaptation of an adaptation. Indeed, the dynamics of translation are particularly evident in this dizzying constellation of texts insofar as the PUG manuscript is a translation at four levels of remove: it is an anonymous Italian version of Ricci's Italian version of Ricci's Chinese version of Eborensis's Latin version adapted from a Latin or Greek text, sometimes by way of Saint Ambrose or Saint Augustine. These transformations at every stage are worthy of extended study.

The BL manuscript is also interesting as a snapshot of an early draft of the essay that is very close, if not identical, to the version that Ricci must have presented to the Prince of Jian'an Commandery. Sometime between 1596 and its republication in the edition of 1599 (now lost) or 1601 (the earliest extant), Ricci decided to add twenty-four new maxims in order to bring the total up to a perfect one hundred. (See "Texts and Variants.") In the process, he seems to have returned to his copy of Eborensis's *Sententiae et exempla* for another dozen aphorisms and to have pillaged his memory for the rest.

But perhaps the most fascinating single feature of the BL manuscript as an early draft of the essay is the way that Ricci identifies himself in the colophon, not least because it sheds light on his early accommodative strategies, but also because it indicates that there were at least two major lines of transmission for the essay. In Feng Yingjing's 馮應京 (1555–1606) edition of 1601, which is the recension later used by Li Zhizao for the standard 1629 collection of *First Writings of Heavenly Studies* (天學初函), the colophon reads, "Compiled by the *moral scholar* from the Great Western Ocean, Li Madou" (大西洋修士利瑪竇集)—where the term *xiushi* 修士 suggests a scholar in training who is devoted to moral self-cultivation.[21] The colophon to the BL manuscript, however, reads, "Compiled by the *mountain recluse* from the kingdoms of the Far West, Li Madou" (太西國山人利瑪竇集)—where the term *shanren* 山人 (literally, "mountain man") refers to a particular type of sage that enjoyed great popularity as a self-designation among freethinking literati in the late Ming.[22] Even though the term was clearly meant to invoke the Han and Song eremitic traditions of Daoist sages in seclusion, in practice the *shanren* of the late Ming were not strictly reclusive but were, on the contrary, frequently entertained as guests in the homes of important people (such as a cousin of the emperor).[23] To be a *shanren* was more an attitude than a style of living in seclusion or in poverty—an attitude of intellectual and aesthetic refinement, and of critical detachment, often against the Confucian norm. Indeed, as the great Li Zhi 李贄 (1527-1602) wittily wrote at the time, the only thing that distinguished a *shanren* 山人 (mountain recluse) from a *shengren* 聖人 (sage) was that the former was lucky enough to be able to write poetry and unlucky enough not to be able to expound the classics, whereas the latter was exactly the opposite.[24]

In the mid-1590s, in what is now a well-known change of missionary tactics, the Jesuits made a crucial decision to alter their accommodative strategy by styling themselves as Confucian literati—that is, as intellectuals in the scholar-official mode. Initially, the Jesuits had adopted the style and clothing of Buddhist monks as socially and spiritually closest to their own religious practices, and even used the Buddhist term *seng* 僧 (priest) to describe who they were and what they did. But Ricci and his confreres eventually became dismayed not only by the disdain with which Buddhist monks were held by many influential people, but also by the passion of Buddhist believers, who seemed devoted to a whole range of superstitious beliefs, convincing the Jesuits that this was the religion that they would most need to oppose if their efforts at widespread conversion to Christianity were to be successful.[25] The BL manuscript, of 1595–1596, corresponds precisely to this period of changing tactics and thus captures a more or less forgotten moment in the history of the mission. In short, between the Jesuits' initial use of the Buddhist *seng* throughout the late 1580s and early 1590s and their use of the Confucian *xiushi* by the turn of the century (later to be replaced by the more common *shenfu* 神父 [spiritual father]), the BL manuscript records Ricci's short-lived and more or less forgotten attempt to fashion his public identity as a *shanren*, or the popular late Ming version of a Daoist sage.

And yet it did not go unnoticed at the time. In the engraver's preface to Ricci's essay in Chen Jiru's famous literary anthology of 1615, Zhu Tingce 朱廷策 (fl. 1610) writes: "From what I have seen of what Mountain Recluse Li has gathered together, the benefits of friendship are great!" (以予所睹利山人集，友之益大哉).[26] Zhu takes it for granted that Ricci is a *shanren*. Indeed, the version of the essay reprinted in Chen's anthology bears an authorial colophon that reads "the mountain recluse, Li Madou" (山人利瑪竇), which suggests that the anthology is closer to Ricci's original text than the standard 1601 text (in which *shanren* does *not* occur) and that the engraver is taking his clue directly from Ricci. Thus it seems that two parallel textual traditions evolved, embodying two slightly different versions of Ricci: the familiar tradition as passed down through Feng Yingjing and Li Zhizao, which seems to represent Ricci's sudden and complete shift from a quasi-Buddhist priest to a Confucian-style scholar, and the other tradition stemming from Ricci's earliest drafts presenting him as a *shanren*, which appears to have reached a significant Chinese readership in the seventeenth century who knew him as such.[27]

Nor was the idea of *shanren* confined solely to the colophon, since Ricci's proem shows signs that he was also subtly fashioning a slightly mystical Daoist identity there, from his initial "choice of residence" in Lingbiao (*bushi* 卜室 suggests a careful decision akin to divination, another meaning of *bu* 卜) to his recognition from a distance that West Mountain must be the "dwelling place of sages" (Ricci surely knew that it was the location of a major Daoist temple, Wanshou Gong 萬壽宮 [Palace of Longevity]), and including his mysteriously feeling compelled to live there ("I could not depart," 不能去). Moreover, Ricci hints at the mountain recluse's emblematic form of reflective retreat when he uses the term *tui* 退 (to retire, withdraw) in describing how he gathered these sayings on friendship for the prince.[28] In Ricci's Italian translation in the BL manuscript, he writes: "I, Matteo, gathered myself for several days in a secret place and gathered everything that I had heard" (Io, Matteo, mi raccolsi per alcuni giorni in luogo secreto e raccolsi tutto quanto avevo udito).[29] Ricci "gathers" both himself and what he had learned in an artful bit of parallelism, but when he embellishes *tui* 退 (to retire) by adding "for several days in a secret place," it is clear that he had imagined a sort of eremitic retreat. We should not make too much of the fact that Ricci also calls his "Doctrine of Friendship" a *you dao* 友道 (or "Dao of Friendship"), since the *dao* of Daoism is properly used for any such system of thought or organized way of doing something, including a religious teaching like Christianity. But all these shades of meaning are potentially lost if we do not recognize Ricci's (at least temporary) self-fashioning as a *shanren*. Indeed, a number of Chinese intellectuals who had heard of Ricci and his writings used other terms with distinctly Daoist connotations to describe him, including *dao ren* 道人 and *dao zhe* 道者—the first of which, as Ricci notes in his journals, even the Jesuits themselves sometimes found it convenient to use in describing themselves to Chinese people in the early to mid-1590s.[30]

But the BL manuscript is also interesting for a single, telling mistake. Ricci notably begins the essay with a flourish of Sinocentrism, introducing himself as: "I, Matteo, from the Far West" (竇也自太西).[31] After all,

Ricci had witnessed the astonishment of Chinese visitors at his eccentric *mappamondo*—and so placing Europe at the far western edge of the world must have seemed like a good place to start making friends in the Middle Kingdom.[32] But in his Italian translation in the BL manuscript, Ricci renders the opening words of the essay as: "Io Matteo dall'ultimo oriente" (I Matteo from the Far East).[33] The mistake is a typical scribal error—a momentary slip as Ricci's eye moved from one page to another in the act of copying—and yet the slip reveals the power of the "Far East" as a structuring idiom and concept. (You can take the Jesuit out of the Far West, but you can't take the idea of the Far East out of the Jesuit.) Moreover, his manuscript opens in the *middle* of the work as it is currently bound, so that to face its opening double pages is to stand at a forking path where the Chinese text leads off to the left and the Italian text leads off to the right: where two Matteos—a "Matteo from the Far West" (竇也自太西) and a "Matteo from the Far East" (Matteo dall'ultimo oriente)—beckon the reader in their respective opposite directions.[34]

Indeed, that chiasmus or crisscrossing of languages and assumed identities may be the perfect emblem for the challenge of reading this Sino-European essay. With its combination of excerpts from classical and patristic sources along with a few uniquely Chinese bits of Ricci's own creatively thrown in, the essay can be read either as a European text translated into Chinese or as a Chinese text composed by a European—it is often difficult to decide which—since at different times it seems one, the other, and both. It is interesting that modern critical responses have tended to split along these very lines into two culturally delineated camps, although naturally there are exceptions to the rule. Non-Chinese scholars have tended to view the essay as a Chinese translation of European originals from such familiar authors as Aristotle, Cicero, Seneca, Plutarch, Herodotus, Augustine, Ambrose, and even Erasmus. In this approach, the work is understood merely as a preliminary step in the Jesuit missionary strategy of accommodation, which actually leaves very little to say about the content. Chinese scholars, however, have mostly concentrated on the content of the essay, which they have tended to view as a personal expression of Ricci's own ideas on friendship combined with other characteristically European or Christian notions that are then sometimes juxtaposed with ideas derived from the Confucian classics, usually with the conclusion that Ricci made friends because his ideas on friendship mostly agree with those of the Confucian tradition—just as Ming readers generally seemed to think. What makes reading this text so challenging and so intriguing is the necessity of taking both paths at once, or at least both paths by turns.

I have not devoted a separate section to European ideas about friendship partly because they are very well represented by Ricci's maxims themselves, and partly because a nuanced treatment is beyond the proper scope of these introductory observations, but a few comments may prove helpful. The ideal of friendship as it was known in the medieval and Renaissance periods in Europe, as largely derived from classical texts, is succinctly summarized by Reginald Hyatte:

> Perfect friendship exists only between virtuous men who love virtue in one another for its own sake; *amici veri* [true friends] are like a single soul in two (or, sometimes, more) bodies; they have all possessions in common, and their affection is reciprocal; their characters, tastes, and opinions are in complete agreement; while growing closer to one another in intimacy,

they also grow in virtue and wisdom that benefit others besides themselves; *vera amicitia* [true friendship], one of the greatest gifts of the gods to man, is worth pursuing and even dying for; it requires a long period of maturation and testing; it lasts for a lifetime and even beyond life; and finally, there are exceedingly few, if any, living examples to which to refer. True friendship has as its primary object not another person but perfect wisdom, goodness, and beauty, which are essentially friendly, benevolent, and beneficent. True friends love these qualities, which they see reflected in their partners.[35]

This idealization of friendship resurfaces throughout Ricci's essay as a formative principle of many maxims, both positively and critically.

One of the aims of this edition is to encourage the sort of nuanced comparative analyses that will articulate the transformations and clashes of such ideas both within and across historical periods and cultural traditions. There is a rich harvest to be gathered here for classicists, sinologists, and comparatists to come.

The remainder of this introduction is devoted largely to the single most important oversight in past studies of the essay—its place in the intellectual and historical context of what one historian has called an "explosion of friendship discourses" in the second half of the Ming dynasty centered around "a cult of friendship among educated males."[36] Everybody, it seems, was talking about friendship at the end of the sixteenth century, especially in southern China, where Ricci was living. In other words, it may not have been that Ricci's ideas on friendship were so very novel to the Chinese, but that the topic itself was perfectly chosen to take full advantage of this intellectual—and political—trend among the educated class. To put it another way, writing such an essay at such a time was the perfect way to make friends among the elite. With this in mind, it comes as no surprise that when Ricci's friend Feng Yingjing had the essay printed in 1601, he recommends it in his short preface as a great way to make friends: "*On Friendship*, with its total of one hundred passages, may serve as an introductory gift when desiring to make friends" (交友論凡百章，藉以為求友之贄).[37] In light of its enormous popularity, it was no doubt used for precisely that purpose in the late Ming.

THE GOLDEN AGE OF FRIENDSHIP

It can be no mere coincidence that the topic of Ricci's first book in Chinese happened to be enjoying a vogue among the educated elite so great that, as the historian Martin Huang puts it, "the late Ming might be considered the golden age of Chinese male friendship," during which some of the "boldest statements and most sophisticated theories of friendship were produced."[38] Ricci's work not only benefited from that wave of popularity, but also was swept up in and became a part of those statements and theories. In addition to having been almost immediately reprinted in collectanea, it was even made one of the primary sources for an anthology on friendship by Zhu Tingdan, whose title—*Guang you lun* 廣友論 (*The Expanded Essay on Friendship*)—seems to play on Ricci's own title.[39] Zhu quotes Ricci's essay fifteen times in the first section, on origins of friendship (友原). Ricci himself notes in his journals that when he met the "famoso letterato" Li Zhi 李贄 (1527–1602) in Nanjing in 1599—that legendary iconoclastic intellectual, a sort of Chinese Giordano Bruno—Li Zhi was so enamored of the essay that he had several copies made for distribution among his students.[40]

To put it simply, Ricci must have known that friendship was hot. And since he had spent the previous four years working on a translation of the Confucian classics, he must have had a fairly good idea about what the Chinese textual tradition had to say on the topic. We cannot know for certain, however, whether he knew anything about the surge of contemporary writings on friendship (he does not mention them) or whether he had any sense that his strange European maxims would be welcomed by the spirit of the age precisely because so many other thinkers in the same region had been boldly redefining that very Confucian tradition on friendship for decades, sometimes in revolutionary ways. The key cultural and institutional factors here were the influence of *jiangxue* 講學 (philosophical debates) and the prevalence of the *jianghui* 講會 (debating societies), which had first been made popular by the Neo-Confucian School of Mind (Xinxue pai 心學派), founded by Wang Yangming 王陽明 (1472–1529), and by its local offshoot, the Taizhou 泰州 school, founded by Wang Gen 王艮 (1483–1541).[41] Historians agree that the precipitous rise of late Ming discourses on friendship was closely related to the resurgence of these debating societies—more or less egalitarian gatherings convened at academies or remote temples in which men would live together for months at a time, fraternizing and engaging in intellectual debate.[42] Once popular in the Song, the *jiangxue* mode of learning became a widespread phenomenon in sixteenth-century China, especially in the south. The men who frequented these societies were forming friendships, to be sure, but what changed the nature of friendship, Huang observes, was that "their sheer eagerness to discourse on friendship and their bold and innovative rhetoric elevated friendship to a moral high ground that it had never occupied before."[43]

In her study of the social culture of the Yangming School of Mind, the Taiwanese historian Lü Miaofen identifies three recurrent themes that arose out of the Ming debating societies and that generally defined the essence of friendship: (1) spiritual reliance (精神的倚靠), or the necessity of friends' relying on one another for the cultivation of virtue and learning; (2) material assistance (物質的資助), or the importance of friends' rendering financial or political support when necessary; and (3) the ideal and practice of seeking friends from all corners of the land (求友四方的理想與實踐), or the importance of searching for true and worthy friends as far away from home as necessary and at any cost.[44] All these ideas have their origins in classical texts, but they took on renewed currency in the late Ming in the culture of the debating societies. The success of Ricci's essay was undoubtedly buoyed by all three of these preoccupations, since all three are expressed therein, often through the circuitous route of a Greek or Roman notion transmuted into a Counter-Reformation value, sometimes via a medieval Christian reformulation and then recast in quasi-Neo-Confucian terms. First, Ricci shows a constant concern with moral questions in his selection of maxims (no great surprise, considering his vocation). Second, Ricci includes a couple of classical-Christian platitudes on the sharing of wealth between friends, which are well represented in Chinese quotations of the essay. Third, and not least: Who had traveled farther in search of worthy friends than the bearded sage from the Far West, Ricci himself?

These three thematic areas of cultivating virtue, sharing wealth, and questing for friends will be discussed in each of the following sections, but it should be stressed at the start that they do not exhaust the discursive field on either the Chinese or the European side. As Lü also describes, the two intellectual obsessions of the Yangming School of Mind that seem to have permeated all philosophical discussions of friendship at the time were (1) a rethinking of the nature of the traditional "five cardinal relationships" (五倫), which could have iconoclastic and potentially revolutionary consequences, and (2) a reevaluation of the Neo-Confucian axiom that "all things form one body" (萬物一體). Ricci's essay contributes absolutely nothing to these two discussions—evidence, perhaps, that he was not trying to adapt his maxims fully to Chinese interests, or perhaps simply that he was cautious about entering into those tricky debates. Ricci's lack of engagement with these issues, however, did not stop some Chinese scholars from reading them into his essay anyway, as we will see in the pages that follow.

The Struts and the Cart: Supporting Virtue in Friendship

One way to approach how Ricci's essay may have bridged the cultural gap between European and Chinese notions of friendship is to examine the hints of how Chinese scholars originally seem to have understood the work. Consider, for example, the response by Li Zhi's famous friend Jiao Hong 焦竑 (1540–1620) in his "Gucheng dawen" 古城答問 (Dialogues from the Ancient City) when answering a question posed by one of his debating society friends, Jin Boxiang 金伯祥:

He [Boxiang] also asked: "When I am at the society, chaotic thoughts do not arise; but when I leave the society, I cannot prevent them from returning. Why is this?" The gentleman replied: "Who taught you to leave? The ancients said: 'One relies on friends to support one's virtue just as the wheel supports and the cart rely on each other. Separate them, and it is hard to move a single step.' Master Li from the Western Regions says: 'A friend is a second I.' His words are wondrously strange but also just."

又問：「吾輩在會時，妄念不起。離卻此會，不免復生。如何？」先生曰：「誰教汝離卻。古人云：以友輔仁，如輔車相依，離之即寸步難行。西域利君言：「友者，乃第二我也。」其言甚奇，亦甚當。[45]

The integration of quotations here is extremely illuminating. The central idea of this passage is that the cultivation of virtue requires the support of friends and that friends are to be found in the debating society: Boxiang's mistake is to assume that he could take his learning with him on his solitary way. The quotation from the "ancients," which carries the main thrust of Jiao Hong's answer, is the second half of one of the most frequently repeated aphorisms on friendship, which was attributed to Zengzi 曾子 in the *Analects*: "The honorable man relies on culture to make friends, and on friends to support his virtue" (曾子曰：君子以文會友，以友輔仁。).[46] The gloss on this passage by the great Song philosopher Zhu Xi 朱熹 (1130–1200) was foundational to the *jiangxue* cult of friendship: "One engages in 'philosophical debate' [*jiangxue*] in order to make friends, and the benefit of the Way becomes clear; one selects the best [friends] in order to strengthen one's humanity, and one's virtue

progresses every day" (講學以會友，則道益明；取善以輔仁，則德日進).[47]
Jiao Hong thus quotes the second half of the line from the *Analects* and
cleverly expands it with an etymological play on the word *fu* 輔, a verb
meaning "to support" but also more anciently a noun for some kind of
supporting piece on either side of a wheeled vehicle. He does this by
quoting a set phrase (*chengyu* 誠語) for the idea of "mutual support" (輔
車相依, "as the cart and the wheel supports need each other"), which
includes the ancient meaning of the word *fu*, and he then extends the
metaphor further with the conclusion that one cannot proceed a single
step in the virtuous life, as in a cart, without such "supports."[48]

Having cited a Confucian classic, Jiao Hong then reinforces his
point by winging forward two thousand years to the newcomer from the
"Western Regions" with a quotation of the first half of the first maxim
from Ricci's treatise ("A friend is a second I"), which goes on to say, "I
must therefore regard my friend as myself" (故當視友如己焉). Thus, in a
stunning gesture, Jiao Hong quotes half of each of the two most influential statements on friendship in the Chinese and European traditions
and combines them as if they were perfectly consonant and complemen-
tary. Jiao Hong praises Ricci's maxim as *qi* 奇, which means something
between "strange" and "beautiful," and as *dang* 當, which could mean
"correct" or "appropriate." But as even the comparison of Jiao Hong's
partial quotation with Ricci's full maxim shows—let alone as it originally appears in Aristotle's *Nicomachean Ethics* or in its Latin rephrasing
in Eborensis's collection—these are clearly not quite the same ideas. In
the European tradition, the notion of identity indicated by the "second
self" carries a sense of equality and mutual respect between friends: it
has nothing *directly* to do with a reliance on friends for the cultivation

of virtue. Indeed, the phrase that a friend is "half of myself" (我之半), which Jiao Hong omits from his quotation (perhaps because it was a little too *qi* for him), alludes to the famous myth attributed to Aristophanes in Plato's *Symposium* of an imaginary origin for humankind in which all people had four arms and four legs and were later split into two halves, forcing them to spend their lives in search of their missing half. In the classic definition from the second-century C.E. lexicon *Shuowen jiezi* 説文 解字 (*An Explanation of Graphs and Analysis of Characters*), which quotes an ancient gloss on the *Book of Rites*, it is said: "Those who have the same teacher are companions; those who have the same will are friends" (同師曰朋，同志曰友).[49] For Jiao Hong, it seems that the identity of the *di er wo* 第二我 ("another I" or "the second me") is understood in a context where one is working side by side with one's companions and friends to cultivate virtue. Indeed, Edward Ch'ien notes that Jiao Hong at times expresses "a strong element of egalitarianism which had been growing in the Wang Yang-ming School of Mind, especially among Chiao Hung's fellow members of the T'ai-chou school," which makes his appropriation of this maxim less surprising.[50] But the nuances are worth stressing, because even though Jiao Hong selected this maxim from Ricci—which is perhaps the most representative maxim in the entire essay of the European discourses on friendship, and certainly the best known in the Renaissance—Jiao Hong seems to have meant something quite different from how Ricci would have understood the same passage. And although it is not difficult to imagine that Ricci would have agreed with Jiao Hong's sentiment, he may have been puzzled by that particular allusion in illustrating the point.

One Rich and One Poor: The Righteousness of Sharing Wealth

The sixteenth century in China saw a surge in philosophical thinking about social organization and the distribution of wealth, which undoubtedly reached its pinnacle, however ill-fated and brief, in the social experiment of He Xinyin's 何心隱 (1517–1579) to reorganize the clan structure of his hometown of Yongfeng 永豐, in Jiangxi Province, into a single commune, which sounds like something straight out of Thomas More's *Utopia* (1516), as well as to found a school called the Collective Harmony Hall (Juhe tang 聚合堂), which was organized on similar principles.[51] An important figure in the Taizhou school, He Xinyin was an unconventional social thinker who was instrumental in reshaping late Ming ideas about friendship, especially in the debating societies. Even though his lasting impact on Chinese social and intellectual culture seems to have been minimal, his thinking made a significant impact on other nontraditional thinkers of the period, such as Li Zhi. The idea that friends ought to render material aid to one another, in the forms of both money and influence for preferment, became a commonplace for discussion, often with the lament that it was an ideal infrequently realized.

Considering the importance of this discourse, it is notable that among the three short pieces that the late Ming writer Xu Bo 徐𤊹 (1570–1642) devotes to friendship in his pen notes, two cite the maxim in Ricci that adapts a similar idea about the sharing of wealth in the *Nicomachean Ethics*:[52]

FRIENDSHIP

The European Li Madou wrote *The True Meaning of the Lord of Heaven*, which people have been reading and discussing, and also *The Essay on Friendship* which especially cuts to the truth of human affairs. There he says: "In ancient times, there were two men walking together, one who was extremely rich, and one who was extremely poor. Someone commented: 'Those two men have become very close friends.' Dou-fa-de retorted: 'If that is indeed so, why is it that one of them is rich and the other poor?'" He also says: "If you see that someone's friends are like a forest, then you know that this is a person of flourishing virtue; if you see that someone's friends are sparse like morning stars, then you know that this is a person of shallow virtue."

交友

利瑪竇歐邏巴人也,著《天主實義》,人傳誦之,而《交友論》尤切中人情。有云:「古有二人同行,一極富,一極貧。或曰:二人為友至密矣。寶法德曰:既然,何一為富者,一為貧者哉?言友之物皆與共也。」又云:「視其人之友如林,則知其德之盛;視其人之友落落,則知其德之薄。」

SHARING WEALTH

I have lamented that, among friends, there is no friendship that involves sharing wealth. All the sages were wise, but I choose Master Yan and Yuan Xian as the wisest. Yan lived in a humble alley with a bamboo scoop for his food and a gourd for his drink; Yuan Xian would eat nine times in thirty days, you could see his elbows when he grasped his lapels, and he had a clay pot for a window and a rope for a door hinge, his poverty was also so extreme.[53] But at the same time Zigong, who was wasteful to the point of selling off his wealth, and who was still the richest man in the states of Cao and Lu, nevertheless assembled a spectacular horse team and carriage to visit Yuan Xian.[54] There was also Gongxi Hua,[55] who extravagantly rode the best horses and wore the finest clothes, and yet at that time he could not share with his two sons even a little. Without experiencing poverty, even a wise man has difficulty recognizing the virtue of sharing wealth through to the end of his life. It is thus excellent that Li Xitai [Ricci][56] in his *Essay on Friendship* says: "There was a poor and a rich man. Someone said: 'They're friends.' Someone else said: 'If they are called friends, why is one poor and the other rich?'"

通財

余嘗嘅朋友，無通財之誼。聖門諸賢，推顏子原憲為最。顏則 簞食瓢飲所居陋巷，原則三旬九食，捉衿見肘，甕牖繩樞，貧亦極矣。乃同時有子貢廢著鬻財，于曹魯之間最為饒益，且結駟連騎以訪原憲。又有公西華乘肥衣輕，當時亦不能分給二子稍稍，不至乏絕，可見通財之義，賢者猶難之，況末世乎。善夫利西泰 《交友論》曰：「一貧一富。或曰：相知。某人曰：既云相知，何為一貧一富哉？」[57]

Citing two of the most popular maxims from Ricci's essay (95 and 61), Xu Bo first suggests that the sharing of wealth is an exemplary ideal among friends, who will be attracted to one another in large numbers (like the trees of a forest) if they possess virtue; but he then goes on to lament that this ideal has never been realized even among Confucius's disciples. The second piece is typical of the rhetoric of writers quoting Ricci, beginning with a series of classical Chinese sources that clearly convey an idea, and then using one of Ricci's maxims at the end for a sort of punch line to clinch it. (The message in Xu Bo's piece is, of course, as much about the usefulness of poverty as about the importance of sharing wealth.)

Ricci's maxim 95 is all the more striking since it repeats another maxim in the essay that expresses exactly the same idea, maxim 29: "The material goods of friends are all held in common" (友之物皆與共). Indeed, Ricci was so intent on stressing the idea that he repeated maxim 29 verbatim as the commentary to maxim 95. Popularized by Erasmus as the first in his blockbuster collection of adages, the idea comes straight out of Aristotle's *Nicomachean Ethics* (and ultimately from Pythagoras and Plato before him)—"The proverb says 'Friends' goods are common property,' and this is correct, since community is the essence of friend-ship"—but the immediate classical source for the little story in maxim 95 and the identity of the mysterious Doufade 竇法德 have long eluded commentators.[58] The BL manuscript, however, offers a rare clue. In his Italian translation there, Ricci renders the name as "Teofrasto," which is probably meant to refer to Aristotle's chief disciple, Theophrastus (b. 370 B.C.E.?), who wrote a lost treatise on wealth.[59] Apparently, Ricci fabri-cated the anecdote of maxim 95 and attributed it to Theophrastus in order to make the most of this European analogue for a value commonly held among Chinese writers on friendship, even if it was not widely practiced at that time either in China or in Europe any more than it is now. Ricci evidently decided that it was more effective to dramatize the idea with a story and a bit of dialogue—worthy of Theophrastus, who was famous in the Renaissance for his collection of *Characters* vividly depicting every type of personality—and Ricci seems to have calculated well, since Chinese writers invariably cite the longer version of maxim 95, even if they feel compelled to make it shorter. If Erasmus influenced his emphasis of the idea, he left no trace of it.

The ultimate classical locus for the idea of *tongcai* 通財 (sharing wealth) is the *Analects* 10.15: "When a friend presented a gift, even if it were a carriage and horses, unless it were sacrificial flesh, [Confucius] would not bow" (朋友之饋，雖車馬，非祭肉，不拜).[60] More specifically, the source for the idea is Zhu Xi's gloss on this passage, which Ricci would surely have known, because the Jesuits relied on editions with Zhu Xi's commentaries to study the Confucian Four Books:

> Among friends there is the righteousness of sharing wealth, for which reason he would not bow even for something as great as a carriage and horses. If it were sacrificial flesh, only then would he bow, in order to show respect to their ancestors just as if they were his own relations. This passage records Confucius's [notion of the] righteousness in friendship.

> 朋友有通財之義，故雖車馬之重不拜。祭肉，則拜者，敬其祖考，同於己親也。 此一節，記孔子交朋友之義。[61]

Zhu Xi's commentary has an important precedent in the Han historian Ban Gu 班固 (32–92), whose Confucian classic *Bai hu tong* 白虎通 (*Discourses in the White Tiger Hall*) may even have provided Zhu Xi's phrase: "The relationship between friends and the proper way of the five constant virtues entail the righteousness of sharing wealth, which is the idea of relieving the poor and helping those in distress" (朋友之際，五常之道，有通財之義，賑窮救急之意).[62]

Ironically, the very same classical source, the *Analects*, was apparently used against Ricci almost two centuries later when the work was excluded from the *SKQS*, as we can infer from the description by the editors of the *Siku quanshu zongmu tiyao* 四庫全書總目提要 (*Synopsis of the Combined Index of the Complete Writings of the Four Treasuries*, 1782, hereafter *SKTY*), who cite the very same two maxims quoted by Xu Bo among their four quotations from Ricci's essay. Since this important bibliographic record has never been translated into a European language before, I offer it here in its entirety:

ESSAY ON FRIENDSHIP, IN ONE VOLUME

Composed by Matteo Ricci, in the *jihai* year of the Wanli period [1599]. Matteo Ricci traveled to Nanchang and discussed the philosophy of friendship with the Prince of Jian'an, as a result of which this compilation was presented as a gift. His words are not deeply unreasonable, and as such most speak about benefit and harm, and are both commonsensical and contradictory mixed together by halves, such as: "The harm from a friend's excessive praise is greater than the harm from an enemy's excessive blame." This conforms to reason. He also says: "If one has many intimate friends, then one has no intimate friends." This shows a profound understanding of the nature of things. He even says: "If one sees that a man's friends are like a forest, then one knows that his virtue is flourishing. If one sees that a man's friends are sparse like morning stars, then one knows that his virtue is thin." This teaches the whole world to make friends indiscriminately. He also says: "If two people become friends, one should not be rich and the other poor." This [shows that he] only understands the "righteousness of sharing wealth" but does not understand the ancient rites: only mourners share wealth;[63] it does not generally apply to all friends. To share wealth as soon as people became friendly with one another would make the rich love without making distinctions, and the poor likewise band together for profit. How could this be the teaching of the *Doctrine of the Mean*? Wang Kentang, in his *Pen Notes from the Lush Ridge Studio*, says: "Master Ricci gave me a copy of the *Essay on Making Friends*. It is delightful the way he expresses it![64] [It gives pleasure to the suffering, and far surpasses Master Mei's *Seven Stimuli*.][65] Even though he has a deep familiarity with Chinese language and literature, it is fitting that we not stop there; therefore I did a little cutting and revising to the essay." Thus the book was punctuated and edited by Kentang.

《交友論》一卷。

明利瑪竇撰,萬曆己亥。利瑪竇遊南昌與建安王論友道,因著是編以獻。其言不甚荒悖,然多爲利害而言醇駁叅半,如云:「友者過譽之害大於讐者過訾之害。」此中理者也。又云:「多有密友,便無密友。」此洞悉物情者也。至云:「視其人之友如林,則知其德之盛。視其人之友落落如晨星,則知其德之薄。」是導天下以濫交矣。又云:「二人爲友,不應一富一貧。」是止知有通財之義而不知古禮。惟小功同財,不槪諸朋友。一相友而即同財,是使富者愛無差等,而貧者且以利合,又豈中庸之道乎? 王肯堂《鬱岡齋筆麈》曰:「利君遺余《交友論》一編,有味哉,其言之也。[病懷爲之爽然,勝枚生《七發》遠矣。]使其素熟於中土語言文字,當不止是,乃稍刪潤著於篇。」則此書爲肯堂所 竄矣。[66]

According to Zhu Xi's commentary on the *Analects*, Confucius found it unnecessary to express gratitude for gifts from friends since he took it for granted that friends ought to share their wealth with one another; and he further explains that when Confucius bowed for sacrificial flesh, he did so out of respect for the ancestors to whom the flesh had been sacrificed, not for the gift itself. The *SKTY* editors, however, invert the sense of that passage by suggesting that the "righteousness of sharing wealth" refers *only* to the ancient rites that govern the sacrifices made during a period of mourning and not to friendship at all—an interpretation that severely limits the scope of gift culture and the bonds that may be created by it. The other maxim that Xu Bo had admired is likewise turned upside down, so that a multitude of friends is no longer proof of someone's virtue but rather a sign of indiscriminate socializing.

Why the sudden shift in judgment? A degree of anti-Jesuit sentiment may be involved, but the shift seems primarily to reflect an increased sensitivity in the eighteenth century to the potential dangers of friendship. Considering the paranoia over dissenting factions and the active suppression of coalitions of friends among the elite under Manchu rule, we should not be surprised to see that a work commissioned by and dedicated to a Manchu emperor would be cautious about a treatise on friendship written by a foreigner.[67] It is especially revealing that the *SKTY* editors judge Ricci's popular essay to be "not deeply unreasonable" when expressing ideas that may *limit* friendships (criticizing friends and keeping their number to a few), but Ricci comes under criticism when praising a multitude of friends or the kind of sharing that may form bonds of indebtedness among congenial groups of wealthy and powerful individuals. Indeed, by breaking down the sharing of wealth into two separate groups, the poor and the wealthy, the analysis in the *SKTY* suspiciously echoes the famous essay by the great Song scholar-official Ouyang Xiu 歐陽修 (1007–1072) on factions, dismissing groups of self-interested petty men as unstable while recognizing the power and durability of friendships formed among *junzi* 君子 (cultivated gentlemen) with common goals—a possibility that the Qing government found genuinely threatening.[68]

In the second half of the Ming, as Lü attests, the influence of Wang Yangming's School of Mind, and especially that of He Xinyin and the Taizhou school, popularized the ideal of rendering material aid to friends—an ideal that was based on classical texts but also represented a rethinking of priorities, in particular about the place of friendship among other social relationships.[69] In the early sixteenth century, Nie Bao 聶豹 (1487–1563) summarized the ancient virtues and responsibilities associated with friendship thus: "Friendship to the ancients [meant] demanding goodness, supporting humane virtue, regulating faults, and sharing wealth" (責善、輔仁、規過、通財，古人之交). In short, friends support with virtue and also with money. Li Zhi held the same ideal and expressed grave disappointment that so few were willing to make sacrifices for He Xinyin when he was in trouble late in life. As Lo Yuet Keung notes, the dramatist and connoisseur Gao Lian 高濂 (*jinshi* 1581) lamented, in his *Zunsheng bajian* 遵生八箋 (*Eight Discourses on the Art of Living*, 1591), that friends in economic distress were treated as strangers in his day, and urged the sharing of wealth, even to the point of wishing "that there would be a Buddhist savior such as the first Chinese Chan patriarch Damo 達摩 [Bodhidharma] coming from the West to save China so that friendship could become what it should be."[70] But this is precisely where we must throw up our hands in defeat when trying to speculate about Ricci's methods, influences, and motivations. We know that Ricci knew the Confucian Four Books, but we have no evidence at all about how much he may have learned from his Chinese tutors or from contemporary literature about the debating societies and their preoccupation with friendship. All we can say is that they were unquestionably factors in the warm reception that the essay received, whether or not Ricci deliberately attempted to fulfill contemporary expectations about the topic.

Friends from Afar: Seeking the World's Best

Among the most memorable words in the entire Confucian canon are the following lines, which open the *Analects*:

> The Master said: "Is it not a pleasure to learn and then to practice often what one has learned? Is it not a joy to have friends come from afar?"

> 子曰：「學而時習之，不亦說乎？有朋自遠方來，不亦樂乎？」[71]

These lines could hardly have been lost on one who had not only studiously translated them into Latin but had also come from afar himself, on a sea journey lasting over four months. The two ideas are presumably related: we study to make ourselves more virtuous, and we are pleased when friends visit us from afar to help us in the process of learning and improving our virtue. Ricci probably also knew the passage in *Mencius* that expands on this idea of the necessity of traveling in order to cultivate virtue with the help of distant friends (in James Legge's famous translation):

The scholar whose virtue is most distinguished in a village shall make friends of all the virtuous scholars in the village. The scholar whose virtue is most distinguished throughout a State shall make friends of all the virtuous scholars of that State. The scholar whose virtue is most distinguished throughout the world shall make friends of all the virtuous scholars of the world.

一鄉之善士，斯友一鄉之善士；一國之善士，斯友一國之善士；天下之善士，斯友天下之善士。[72]

In short, one travels farther for the better friends. But what Ricci may not have known is that what first appeared in *Mencius* as an ideal of selectiveness in seeking suitable companions later found expression in the debating society culture of the sixteenth century as the imperative to leave one's home and family from time to time in order to engage in philosophical debate with like-minded intellectuals in remote locations. This passage from *Mencius* was frequently quoted by Ming intellectuals in their discussions of friendship, including Luo Hongxian 羅洪先 (1504–1564), Feng Congwu 馮從吾 (1557–1627), and Gu Xiancheng 顧憲成 (1550–1612)—and it was especially important to Wang Ji 王畿 (1498–1583), in whose writing, as Huang puts it, "traveling and making friends are inseparable activities."[73]

Moreover, as Lü puts it, for many scholars of the late Ming, the notion of "the best scholars under heaven" (天下之善士) was more than just an ideal: it was a practical way of life.[74] Both Lü and Huang describe the recent work of historians showing that the booming trade economy of the Ming combined with a strong infrastructure to increase the ease of travel on an unprecedented scale, for both business and leisure.[75] In short, as Huang argues throughout his study, the Ming became a traveling culture, and the importance of this new way of life to the renewed value placed on friendship was continually reenacted by scholars who participated in the debating societies.

Ricci makes it no secret that he has come from afar. Let us recall the opening line of the essay:

> I, Matteo, from the Far West, have sailed across the seas and entered China with respect for the learned virtue of the Son of Heaven of the Great Ming dynasty as well as for the teachings bequeathed by the ancient kings.

> 竇也，自太西，航海入中華，仰 大明天子之文德，古先王之遺教。

The ingredients are all there: he has come from afar (the "Far West") looking for learning (*wen* 文) and virtue (*de* 德). And yet one cannot help but feel that Ricci is not exactly laboring the point here. If Ricci was indeed trying to hint that he had traveled from the Far West as among the best scholars under heaven in search of the best scholars under heaven, he did so very modestly. But it is also possible that Ricci was doing nothing of the kind, and that it was his friend and "publisher," Feng Yingjing, who in his own preface picked up the unintentional connection and stressed it for Ricci's readers:

> Master Xitai [Ricci], in an arduous journey of 80,000 *li*, has traveled eastwardly into China in order to make friends. Because his understanding of the way of friendship is deep, he is urgent in his entreaties and steadfast

with his companions; and he discourses on the way of friendship in surprising detail. Ah, isn't it great what friendship binds together!

西泰子間關八萬里，東遊於中國，為交友也。其悟交道也深，故其
相求也切，相與也篤，而論交道獨詳。嗟夫，友之所繫大矣哉！[76]

Without actually alluding to Confucius or Mencius, Feng makes the
connection clear by stating what Ricci himself never explicitly says and
would probably not have said, since it was not strictly true: that Ricci has
come to China from across the world in order to make friends like any
other devotee of debating society culture. Indeed, the prominent historian Nicolas Standaert observes that one of the objections voiced against
the Jesuits in Chinese writings was that they had not really come from
thousands of *li* away, as they claimed, and that such claims were merely
a strategy for gaining respect.[77] Nonetheless, even if Ricci did not try to
style himself after the Mencian ideal, readers in the late Ming could not
help but see him thus—whether or not they liked what they saw.

Filling the Gap: Friendship Among the Wulun

In his discussion of anti-Jesuit writings in Chinese, Standaert identifies
a criticism even worse than the Jesuits' supposedly lying about their origins: "The most serious criticism against the Jesuits was that they did not
enter into the five basic human relationships (*wulun* 五倫): they do not
marry, therefore they neglect the relation of husband and wife (夫婦); they
leave home, thus the relationships with their parents (父母) and brothers
(兄弟) are broken; and by leaving their country they lose the relationship

with their ruler (君臣), so that only the relationship with friends (朋友) remains."[78] To be sure, the most surprising feature of Ricci's essay when read in a Ming intellectual context is that, whereas Chinese writings on friendship are almost obsessively concerned with the status of friendship among the *wulun*, Ricci nowhere mentions these relationships. The omission is all the more surprising since Aristotle, in book 7 of the *Nicomachean Ethics*, also compares friendship with the relationships of father and son, ruler and subject, and husband and wife, a text Ricci must have known well since he independently drew a few ideas from it that do not come by way of Eborensis's commonplace book. One is tempted to speculate that Ricci may have intentionally steered away from the topic altogether in order not to be embroiled in controversial debates about the *wulun* challenging the status quo, or perhaps even to avoid drawing attention to his own strategy of seeking to advance the mission by making influential friends—a tactic that could have come under criticism as the sort of favoritism or corruption all too prevalent in the period. Whatever his motivation may have been, his complete avoidance of the *wulun* did not prevent others from reading it into the essay anyway.

In a watershed article, Hsü Dau-lin has argued that the fundamental social concept of the *wulun* was first mentioned not by Confucius or his immediate disciples, but two generations later in *Mencius*, and that it was not even defined as it is currently understood until the Song dynasty, when the Neo-Confucian school drew on certain Han writings from the Yin-Yang school and redefined what had originally been the two reciprocal relationships of duty between father and child and that between ruler and king, and expanded them to the current configuration of four hierarchical bonds and one egalitarian bond.[79] Be that as it may, there has been an emerging consensus among historians that friendship has always been considered dangerous either to one's self or to the Confucian order represented by the other four relationships. David Nivison's early work has shown how anxiety about political factions under the Qing was aroused by groups of elite men whose rhetoric of friendship unnervingly echoed that of Ouyang Xiu's 1044 essay on factions, in which the idea of *tongxin* 同心 (common heart-and-mind) applies to both friends and political allies.[80] Norman Kutcher has demonstrated that ideas about friendship have always been seen as a threat to the stability of the other relationships, from their first appearances in early Confucian writings to their full-blown discussions in Song Neo-Confucian writing.[81] And Joseph McDermott has argued that Zhu Tingdan's 1626 anthology on friendship—*Guang you lun*, which cites Ricci more than a dozen times— was actually a covert criticism of a corrupt court and bureaucracy, and of a disengaged and ineffective emperor, by means of its sustained emphasis on the bond of friendship over the bond of sovereign and subject.[82]

From a comparative context, we could observe, as Alan Bray has pointed out, that the chief difference between traditional European conceptions of friendship and our modern sense of friendship is that whereas we now think of friendship as a positive and private matter, for-merly "friendship was *dangerous* because it signified in a public sphere."[83] Beyond the well-known idealistic discourses in philosophical writings, one's "friends" represented one's power of influence in a continuum of spheres from the family to the state. Broadly speaking, then, traditional European notions seem to have been much more similar to traditional Chinese ideas than our modern notions are. But the fundamental dif-ferences appear along the fault lines of the *wulun*. In sixteenth-century

Europe, *friend* had a readily available metaphorical function encompassing a variety of relationships, including even that of a suitor or a lover in addition to that with family members, and could be used even to describe one's relationship with God (something more or less inconceivable in Chinese discourse); within the traditional structure of the *wulun*, however, friendship stood apart from them all as radically different.[84]

Admittedly, sometimes Chinese discourses on friendship take on an apparently rather conservative cast, such as in the opening remarks of the Song dynasty writer Li Zhiyan 李之彥 (fl. 1228–1268) in his piece *Pengyou* 朋友 (*Friends*):

> "The honorable man relies on culture to make friends, and on friends to support his virtue." The one who befriends another befriends his virtue. When they are very close, they hold each other's hands and speak what is in their hearts, which must certainly cause the relationships between sovereign and subject, father and son, older brother and younger brother, and husband and wife to be manifested purely in complete correctness. This is the first righteous principle of friendship.

> 君子以文會友，以友輔仁。友之者，友其德也。當親密之時，握手論心，必使君臣父子之倫，兄弟夫婦之倫，粹然一出於正。此交友第一義也。[85]

(Note the quotation from the *Analects*.) This passage clearly indicates that friendship is subordinated to the other four relationships and that its proper aim is their cultivation and stability, but one can see how easily a subversive reading could suggest that friendship is primary and that its foundation and form will determine the other four relationships in whatever way virtue dictates. Indeed, as a nonhierarchical bond, friendship always posed the problem of definition and categorization in relation to the other four, and that tension seems never to have been far from the minds of Ming writers on the subject. Consider this ancient anecdote from Liu Xiang's 劉向 (77 B.C.E.–6 C.E.) *Shuo yuan* 説苑 (*Garden of Stories*), as retold by the great Ming essayist Zhang Dai 張岱 (1597–1689) in his *Ye hangchuan* 夜航船 (*Night Ferry*):

"When a friend is right and the prince disagrees." King Xuan of Zhou was about to have his minister Du Bo executed, but he was innocent of any crime. Bo's friend Zuo Ru remonstrated with the king on nine occasions, but the king would not listen. The king said: "You are contradicting the prince and following friends." Bo replied: "If the prince is right and one's friend disagrees, then the prince should execute the friend; if one's friend is correct and the prince disagrees, then it is proper for the friend to depart from the prince." The king executed Du Bo, and Zuo Ru died.

友道君逆。周宣王將殺其臣杜伯，而非其罪。伯之友左儒爭之于王，九复之，而王不聽。王曰：「汝別君而導友也。」儒曰：「君道友逆，則順君以誅友；友道君逆，則順友以違君。」王殺杜伯，左儒死。[86]

The anecdote pits the relationship between friend and friend against the relationship between prince and subject—and it cuts both ways. It raises the possibility not only of corrupt and even revolutionary coalitions between friends who are so devoted to each other that they would repeatedly remonstrate with a ruler, and even die (of a broken heart, it seems) at the other's unjust execution, but also of the sort of tyrannical authority that may incite the forming of such alliances (Du Bo's innocence makes this point clear, even if the story seems to stress the futility of resisting power, at least through direct remonstrance).

But even when far from the seditious, a number of Ming intellectuals were actively involved in challenging the social and political status quo in many different ways. Wm. Theodore de Bary has observed that in Li Zhi's encomium of He Xinyin, in *Fenshu* 焚書 (*A Book to Be Burned*), Li writes that "of the five Confucian relations," He "discarded four and kept only the relation between friend and friend"; and that when Li praised He at this moment "he was also speaking for himself," since "in his discussion of human relationships Li attached the greatest importance to the relation of friendship, which for him tended to supersede all others."[87] The audacity of this idea is the very inversion of the traditional hierarchy, which always places friendship beneath the other relationships, even when it is considered a necessary supplement.

Huang's survey of late Ming figures associated with debating societies shows how crucial discussions of this sort were to the formation of that culture and to the cult of friendship. Huang notes that Gu Xiancheng, an influential member of the Donglin 東林 (Eastern Grove) movement and an active participant in philosophical debating, even went so far as to favor debating societies as a place devoted to friendship and its well-known virtues over the *dangers* of the "family (*jiating* 家庭) with its cozy and indulging atmosphere as a place where one could easily experience moral degeneration (*zui yi duoluo* 最易墮落)."[88] For Gu, friendship was the model for the other four relationships, another inversion of the traditional hierarchy with potentially radical implications.[89] Huang also describes a passage on friendship by "a relatively obscure late Ming scholar" named Gu Dashao 顧大韶 (b. 1576), who, in a work called *Fangyan* 放言 (*Daring Words*), claims that friendship is based on *zhenxin* 真心 (true heart), whereas the relationships of father and son and sovereign and subject are based on *renqing* 人情 (common sentiments and social conventions) and *mingjiao* 名教 (Confucian teachings on social order and ritual), respectively, concluding that "friendship is the most important because it possesses the ultimate power of transcendence (it never dies since it comes from the heart) that the other two traditionally important relationships do not have."[90] Regardless of whether Ricci knew about such discourses, it is notable that in the one place where he veers closest to the topic, maxim 50, "Friends surpass family members in one point only . . ." (友於親，惟此長焉), Ricci seems to have emphasized the "only" (*wei* 惟), since his source for this maxim in Cicero does not have that qualification.[91] Ricci's formulation is far from the daring words of Gu Dashao's in expressing a similar sentiment.

Yet, despite Ricci's avoidance of these issues, once again Chinese readers seem to have read the essay as a contribution to these discussions. We saw earlier how Feng Yingjing began his preface to the 1601 edition by marveling that Ricci had traveled 80,000 *li* to make friends; Feng's very next words are:

> Between sovereign and subject, there must be justice; between father and son, there must be affection; between husband and wife, there must be difference; between older and younger brother, there must be order. How, then, could there be no friendship?

君臣不得不義，父子不得不親，夫婦不得不別，兄弟不得不序。是
烏可無交？[92]

As vapid as the point may be, Feng quickly offers the obligatory connection of friendship to the established discourse on the *wulun*, as Ricci
himself had failed to do. Others, however, do it with more panache.

It may be an indication of how completely Ricci's essay has been iso-
lated from studies on Ming friendship that two of the most accomplished
historians of the topic have both discussed a notable passage from Zhu
Tingdan's *Guang you lun* without recognizing that it had been excerpted
from a preface added to Ricci's essay written by the famous editor and
preface writer Chen Jiru when he reprinted it in his celebrated collectanea in 1615.[93] The philosophical terms of Chen's preface render it rather
difficult to understand, but because of Chen's prominence as an editor,
and because it has never been translated before, I offer it here in its entirety (the passage excerpted by Zhu Tingdan is in italics):

SHORT PREFACE TO THE *ESSAY ON FRIENDSHIP*
That which stretches out becomes a god; that which bends becomes a
demon. *In the relationships of sovereign and subject, father and son, husband
and wife, older brother and younger brother, there is respectful service. The
human spirit bends in the relationships of sovereign and subject, father and
son, husband and wife, older brother and younger brother, but it stretches out in
friendship. It is like spring moving within the flowers or the wind and thunder
moving within the primordial energy. The four relationships are not complete
without friendship.* Surprisingly, Master Li from the western seas saw this.
Although Master Li is learned in the diagrams of the three subjects[94] of

heaven, earth, and humanity, his studies are only to serve the Lord of Heaven. And he does not discuss at all any of the teachings of the Sinicized Buddha[95] and of Laozi. But as for Heaven, who can do without people? A friend is thus the most suitable companion for a person. Zhu Mingchang,[96] from Zuili,[97] who has the attitude of the ancients toward making friends, engraved this book, which truly can fill in what Zhu Mu and Liu Xiaobiao did not provide. We should each place a copy at our side in order to warn those who make friends like flocks of crows assembling.

By Chen Jiru, [or] Zhongchun.

友論小敍

伸者為神，屈者為鬼。君臣父子夫婦兄弟者，莊事者也。人之精神，屈於君臣父子夫婦兄弟，而伸於朋友。如春行花內，風雷行元氣內。四倫非朋友不能彌縫。不意西海人利先生乃見此。利先生精於天地人三才圖。其學惟事天主為教，凡震旦浮屠老子之學，勿道也。夫天，孰能舍人哉？人則朋友其最耦也。 檇李朱銘常， 於交道有古人風， 刻此書。 真可補朱穆劉孝標之未備。吾曹宜各置一通於座隅， 以告世之烏合之交者。

仲醇陳繼儒題 。[98]

Chen depicts friendship here as an essential supplement that completes or "fills in the crevices" (*mifeng* 彌縫) among the other four relationships, just as Ricci's essay makes up for or mends (*bu* 補) what is missing in the sayings on social relationships in the works of such ancient writers as Zhu Mu 朱穆 (100–165) and Liu Jun 劉峻 (462–521).[99] High praise, indeed, despite what feel like reservations about Ricci's emphasis on the heavenly. But the praise of friendship is even more intense than that.

The opening line of Chen's preface makes an abstruse allusion to Zhu Xi's *Zhongyong zhangju* 中庸章句 (*Annotations on "The Doctrine of the Mean"*), in which Zhu Xi explains that when both kinds of *qi* 氣 (material energy) are present, then the *gui* 鬼 (demons) have a *yin* 陰, or female, essence, and the *shen* 神 (gods) have a *yang* 陽, or male, essence; but that when there is only one kind of *qi* present, then it becomes a *shen* when it moves forward to perfection and stretches out, but it becomes a *gui* when it doubles back and retreats, even though both are still of a single substance (愚為以二氣言，則鬼者陰之靈也，神者陽之靈也。以一氣言，則至而伸者為神，反而歸者為鬼，其實一物而已).[100] In other words, the "bending" required of the four hierarchical bonds likens them to demons, as opposed to the free-flowing *qi* found in the godlike friendship. By omitting that opening line from his quotation of Chen's preface, Zhu Tingdan obscures the full sense of the metaphor (although it is, admittedly, rather difficult to grasp anyway), which bases its analogy of the place of friendship in the *wulun* on the fundamental forces of material energy in the universe. What remains of the metaphor still makes a certain sense, but what is perhaps most striking is Chen's claim (also omitted by Zhu Tingdan) that "Master Li . . . saw this" (利先生乃見此), attributing to him an understanding of the cosmic significance of the interrelations of the *wulun* that is really not comparable to anything in Ricci's essay. (And the idea is compelling enough to Zhu Tingdan as a reader for him to quote it on page 3 of a four-volume anthology on friendship, even though he cuts the mention of Ricci.) In other words, whether Ricci actually tried to accommodate European ideas about friendship to what he thought might appeal to Chinese readers, his essay was nonetheless inserted into a preexisting discourse on friendship, notwithstanding fundamental differences between the two.

Even more surprising, perhaps, is that the Jesuits did not take the hint. Half a century later, when Martino Martini wrote his sequel to Ricci's popular text with his own treatise on friendship, he expanded at great length on a number of ideas but made no effort whatsoever to integrate any of his new work into the ubiquitous Chinese categories of the *wulun*. As in Ricci's case, it was left to a Chinese friend to do it for him, one Zhang Anmao 張安茂, who gives the work a proper opening with a preface that begins: "Four of the five relationships are founded by heaven, leaving only friendship to be founded by people" (夫五倫之四皆本乎天，獨朋友則本乎人).[101]

In the late twentieth century, a wonderful discovery was made in a manuscript collection in Saint Petersburg of two private and probably never-published prefaces from the seventeenth century on Ricci's essay and Martini's longer treatise.[102] Both these fascinating prefaces also explicitly situate the Jesuit texts in relation to the *wulun*. Translated by Giuliano Bertuccioli in the excerpts that follow, the first preface, by Shen Guangyu 沈光裕 (*jinshi* 1640), treats Martini's essay alone; it begins:

> Friendship is what is conferred upon us by God and therefore is one of the five relationships. The five relationships mutually complete and interpenetrate each other, but friendship does so more completely and in greater depth. So indispensable is friendship to the others and such is the value of its example that we can never express it in words, never finish reading it in writing, never conceive it with our mind. If we were to examine the

relationships of sovereign and subject, father and son, husband and wife, elder and younger brother one by one, we would soon discover that friendship is superior to all, as its Way is incommensurably great and singularly splendid [而友義逾著，交道洋為大].[103]

The praise of friendship rivals the most radical redefinitions that we saw earlier in the likes of Li Zhi, He Xinyin, and Gu Dashao. The second of the unpublished prefaces, by Liu Ning 劉凝 (ca. 1625–1715), was written for a private copy of both essays bound together; it begins:

I have copied together and given the place of honor on my desk to the "Essay on (Making) Friendship," written by Mister Li Xitai [Ricci] and the "Treatise on (Searching for) Friendship," written by Mister Wei Jitai [Martini], so that I can read them aloud. These two gentlemen, who have abandoned their country and left their relatives in search of friends ninety thousand miles from home, can be said to be sincere and trustworthy. . . . If the four relationships do not find rapid completion they will not find their right place in the future. This is why friendship is so important [非惟無以勤四倫之成，將四倫俱不得其所，此友誼重也].[104]

In both these cases, as in so many others, the Jesuit discourses on friendship are seen to contribute to the valorization of friendship over and above the other four cardinal relationships in a formulation setting it against those four in order to improve them by compensating for their inherent deficiencies. (Note also that Liu stresses the great distance that Ricci has traveled to make friends, in the Mencian tradition.) As we saw at the beginning of this section, considering that the Jesuits conspicuously failed to meet the strict Confucian expectations of respecting the other four relationships (at least by a hostile judgment), Ricci may well have thought his position too hazardous to enter explicitly into debates that he knew to be critical of the relationships that he and his fellow Jesuits had supposedly abandoned. But Ricci's apparent refusal to adopt the terms of this discussion may demonstrate only the limits of his accommodative practices, or perhaps simply a desire to present classical European wisdom rather than to dabble amateurly in relatively unknown territory.

MATTEO SAYS: TRANSLATING THE MASTER

The interpretative challenge Ricci's essay poses arises out of the difficulty of the genre itself: How does one read a collection of more or less translated maxims introduced by an autobiographical proem? The two parts seem contradictory, almost mutually exclusive. As adaptations of the writings of other people, such maxims would seem to be impersonal while having been chosen, presumably, to echo the sentiments of the author; and yet, as so many separate items, they seem to resist narrative coherence while at the same time appearing to suggest a kind of story to be read between the lines. Moreover, Ricci presents all his maxims with no attribution whatsoever, which may be one reason that so many readers (especially Chinese scholars) seem to want to discover in the beloved essay a window onto the mind of this famous friend to China, and why European scholars (most of whom are Christians or even Jesuits themselves) have tended to dismiss the essay less warmly, as a derivative, secular text, a mere pastiche of common authors.

In his popular hagiographic biography, Vincent Cronin describes the essay, in a turn of circular logic, as the very emanation of Ricci's amicable character: "Ricci prized nothing in life so much as seeking and making friends spontaneously. Time and again he had been hurt when his overtures had foundered on the rock of xenophobia. By writing such a work he fulfilled his own affectionate nature and hoped to dispel one of the chief obstacles to missionary progress. The book took the form of a dialogue."[105] In other words, Ricci wrote this essay—in "the form of a dialogue"—because he loved to make friends, the proof of which is that he wrote this essay. Among the various misconceptions about the relatively unknown essay frequently repeated in scholarship, some are inconsequential and easy to dispel, such as that it contains differing numbers of maxims or that it was reprinted in collectanea in which it does not, in fact, appear.[106] But the idea that it is a dialogue is so frequently repeated and has become so commonplace that most readers who have heard of Ricci's essay on friendship probably believe that, as one of the most prominent historians of Christianity in China once put it, "Ricci wrote a dialogue in imitation of Cicero's treatise *De Amicitia*."[107] The relative unavailability of the text before now has undoubtedly contributed to this misconception, but there is more to it than that, I believe; and the explanation of how this idea arose sheds light on the interpretation—and translation—of the essay.

As I mentioned in a previous section, Ricci invented a slight literary fiction for his proem in which the Prince of Jian'an Commandery expresses a desire to know more about European ideas on friendship. In his journals, Ricci comfortably admits that he was "pretending" (*fingendo*) to have had such a conversation, but his fellow Jesuits evidently felt some anxiety about the story. When Nicolas Trigault prepared Ricci's Italian journals for posthumous publication in 1615 by heavily editing them and translating them into Latin, Trigault added a parenthetical statement: "Father Matteo pretended (as indeed Cicero had done in his *Laelius*) to be questioned by the king."[108] In a subtle defense of Ricci's pretense, Trigault thus reminds readers that Cicero himself had invented a similar fiction for his treatise on friendship. Later, when Louis Gallagher translated Ricci's journals into English in the 1950s for what is still the most widely available version, not only did he use Trigault's Latin version (which added the parenthetical reference to Cicero) instead of Ricci's original Italian, but he also silently removed the conspicuous word *pretended*, so that it reads simply: "like Cicero in his *Lelius*, Father Matthew is being questioned by the King."[109] Thus through a series of slight mistranslations, Ricci's essay (as if by his own declaration) has been transformed into a dialogue like Cicero's. But, in fact, Ricci had described only the pretended request from the prince as a dialogue, not the work as a whole, which is, of course, a series of maxims. Indeed, in Chinese terms, the essay is a *zalun* 雜論 (miscellany treatise), a collection of excerpted passages with a perfectly typical short preface explaining the circumstances of their preparation—just as it was classified in the early eighteenth century by the editors of the imperial collectanea *TSJC*.

If the consequences of this series of slips were merely the occasional misreporting of the genre of the work, it would hardly be worth mentioning; but the misconception seems to have had a profound influence on the assumptions of readers, contributing to the belief that the essay is a personal expression of Ricci's own ideas about friendship. Indeed, when the modern Chinese translator of Ricci's complete works, Luo Yu 羅漁, translates (rather freely) the description in Ricci's journals just discussed, he makes the predictable next misstep: not only does he plainly say that "the book was written in the form of questions and answers" (本書是以問答方式寫成), but he also says that "it consists entirely of the views of famous people both ancient and modern, with the addition of opinions from the Catholic Church fathers, and even Master Ricci's own personal thoughts" (都是古今名人的見解，加上天主教教父們的意見，以及利氏個人的心得).[110] Luo is supposedly translating or paraphrasing the same passage in Ricci's journals here, but the interpolation of Ricci's "own personal thoughts" comes entirely out of Luo's imagination of what the essay must contain.

In a Chinese context, this association of a dialogue with the personal thoughts of a master is undoubtedly reinforced by the example of the *Lunyu* 論語 (*Analects*)—that famous collection of conversations with Confucius consisting of questions and answers, traditionally believed to have been posthumously gathered and recorded by his disciples. Moreover, when Ricci's essay appears in the early collectanea of the Ming and Qing, the proem is usually cut, which is where Ricci explains that the work is compiled from the sayings of others; and most of those collectanea begin with the phrase "Li Madou says" (利瑪竇曰). In a recent article, one modern scholar even introduces every quotation from Ricci's essay with the archaic formula "Master Li says" (利子曰), making him sound very much like Confucius indeed.[111]

In a European context, however, the confusion is undoubtedly due to the fact that the most famous treatise on friendship during the Renaissance really was written in the form of a dialogue: Marcus Tullius Cicero's (106–43 B.C.E.) *Laelius de amicitia* (*Laelius on Friendship*), which consists largely of an extended discourse punctuated by very short prompts from other speakers. In that work, Cicero gives evidence of the elusive nature of the genre by explaining in his own preface that he has invented a conversation with Gaius Laelius (fl. 204–160 B.C.E.), who was famous for his heroic friendship with Scipio Africanus (235–183 B.C.E.), in which he has attributed to Laelius a combination of Cicero's own ideas on friendship mixed together with those of Laelius himself as they had been reported to him by Laelius's son-in-law decades after Laelius's death. Reading Cicero's dialogue, it is thus impossible to know which ideas were originally Laelius's and which Cicero's. Ultimately, the question thus comes down to one of the most elementary and irresolvable questions of literary hermeneutics: Exactly how much of the meaning of a text can we attribute to the author's own experiences, beliefs, and intentions; and how much should we attribute to literary fiction, convention, the influence of other sources, or even our own needs and desires?

Interestingly, the desire to view the essay as an expression of Ricci's personal sentiments seems to be the very method of one of the only critical studies of the work available in English by a Chinese scholar, which appeared in the premier journal of sinological mission studies, *Monumenta Serica*.[112] The author begins by claiming that the essay must surely reveal "Ricci's prior frustration and lack of Chinese friendship," since, at the (fictional) prompting of his princely host, Ricci (as the author argues) would have "selected passages and aphorisms that would seem fitting to his personal experience in China thus far. Hence, it is understandable that Ricci seemed to look at the essay as a personal 'dialogue' between him and his host."[113] (Note how the ideas of personal expression and the dialogue form are intertwined.)

The author of this study then recounts an incident from the journals in which Ricci felt betrayed by someone he considered a friend (a local official who later distanced himself from Ricci when the Jesuits fell under general suspicion), after which the study proceeds by quoting maxim after maxim, followed by a hopeful assertion that each one must express how Ricci felt about friendship, such as the following:

> Although Ricci claimed that he was merely culling from Western sources on friendship, his emotive presence in the project was strongly visible. Occasionally he would even include his personal experience of negotiating with Chinese people in the essay. For instance, he says in one passage, "I once met a worthy friend by chance, even though the meeting was brief as slapping each other's hands, it was nonetheless beneficial to me, because he was affined to my aspiration to goodness." It is not clear to whom Ricci referred in this passage, but it is possible that it was someone he had met in China.[114]

The wishful thinking that such a reading method expresses is that Ricci's essay arises directly out of his contact with Chinese people. But the impasse that the essay presents is of how to know whether a particular passage reflects Ricci's "emotive presence" or his "personal experience," or whether, on the contrary, he simply thought that Plutarch had a particularly pithy passage worth paraphrasing. The implications are serious, since the assumed context of Ricci's "personal experience" here skews the interpretation and translation of this maxim (number 68), which I translate in more general terms:

If, by chance, I happen to encounter a wise friend, even if we only clap hands once and part, it is never so little that it does not reinforce my will to do good.

吾偶候遇賢友，雖僅一抵掌而別，未嘗少無裨補以洽吾為善之志也。

The grammatical and syntactical structures of classical Chinese are permissive enough that both these translations are linguistically defensible (the past tense of a particular action or the present tense of a universal condition), but the divergent results arise from completely different assumptions about the context, function, and intention of Ricci's text. These differences explain why the other translation strangely reverses the action of the final clause, so that instead of the speaker having his "will to do good" augmented or reinforced (裨補) by the friend (as I render it), in the other version it is the *friend* who is "affined" to the speaker's "aspiration to goodness." Ricci is thus imagined as walking the streets of Nanchang spreading his gospel of goodness with high fives.

It is more likely, however, as the classicist Sofia Maffei has pointed out in her supplementary work on Ricci's sources, that the maxim is derived from a section of Plutarch's *Moralia*, "To Discern a Flatterer from a Friend," that was well known in the Renaissance.[115] The passage in question describes true friends as those who do not strain to ingratiate themselves, but who instead express their friendship casually (here quoted from the famous 1603 translation of Philemon Holland [1552–1637]): "And verily as friends many times when they meet one another in the street, passe by without good-morrow or god-speed, or any word at all between them; onely by some lightsome looke, cheerefull smile, or amiable regard of the eie reciprocally given and taken, without any other token els, there is testified the good-will and mutual affection of the heart within."[116] Of course, Ricci has adapted Plutarch's "cheerefull smile, or amiable regard of the eie" (that is, a wink) to a *dizhang* 抵掌 (clapping or slapping of the palms), perhaps in order to make the quick greeting more plausible to Chinese readers. But, more important, Ricci has changed the idea of a quick but sincere expression of friendliness to the idea of how one's moral resolve can be strengthened by a brief encounter with a wise friend. In a sense, Ricci has made the idea from Plutarch more intelligible to his Chinese readers insofar as the ideal of Chinese friendship was one of mutual assistance in the cultivation of virtue, as I discussed in a previous section. Fortunately, since this maxim is among the original seventy-six of his first draft, it appears in the Italian translation Ricci drafted and sent to Rome, as it survives in the recently rediscovered British Library manuscript, as follows:

Every time I meet a good friend, even if it be no more than for the space of a slap of the hand, I never fail to perceive something useful for increasing my virtue.

[Tutte le volte che mi accosto ad alcun buon amico benche non sia piu che per spatio di una battuta di mano, mai lasciai di udire alcuna cosa utile per aumentare in me la virtu.][117]

However "authoritative" (by definition) Ricci's translations are, we must bear in mind that they still offer but one among what are sometimes multiple possible meanings—one, in particular, that seems intended to direct his fellow Jesuits in Europe toward concepts that will be easier for them to understand or accept—which consideration should urge us to be cautious in our approach to those translations; but in this case, it seems safe to say that Ricci also seems to have envisioned the maxim in more general terms, rather than as a recollection of an actual encounter with a Chinese friend.

All this is not to insist that Ricci never felt dissatisfied with the behavior of those he called friends, or that he never wrote a maxim that expressed his true feelings or experiences about friendship—indeed, it is almost impossible not to see a few of them in that light (for example, see maxims 26, 27, and 74). But we must beware of a wholesale transformation of the essay into a biographical work, even while toying with those possibilities, not least since it will affect how we translate and interpret the text.

CONCLUSION: FRIENDS NEAR AND FAR

In conclusion, let us return, in the opening lines of the *Analects*, to the singular joy of having a friend visit from afar: "Is it not a pleasure to learn and then to practice often what one has learned? Is it not a joy to have friends come from afar?" As I mentioned in a previous section, Ricci seems not to have tried very conspicuously to make use of these lines to style himself as one of the best scholars of the world searching for friends among the other best scholars of the world, even though at least some Chinese readers clearly understood his comments that way. Nevertheless, it is certain that Ricci took note of Zhu Xi's commentary on that very passage, which repeats a gloss of Zengzi's explaining that *yue* 説 (happiness) is felt within the heart, whereas *le* 樂 (joy) is primarily expressed outwardly ([程子]又曰：「説在心，樂主發散在外」).[118]

This detail is important because it explains an otherwise mysterious opposition in maxim 54 (my italics): "When vulgar friends meet, their *joy* is greater than their *happiness*; and when they part, they have a lingering sense of unease. When virtuous friends gather, their *happiness* is greater than their *joy*; and after they depart, there is no feeling of shame" (俗友者同而樂多於悦，別而留憂；義友者聚而悦多於樂，散而無愧). The difficulty of this maxim is that it hinges entirely on the difference articulated by Zengzi and Zhu Xi between *le* 樂 (joy) and *yue* 説/悦 (happiness) as exterior and interior pleasures, respectively. Ricci's own translation in the British Library manuscript shows that he had precisely this distinction in mind: "When lowly friends are together their exterior happiness is greater than their interior" (Gli amici triviali quando stanno insieme la allegrezza exteriore he maggiore che l'interiore).[119] In creating this maxim, Ricci evidently took this classical lexical opposition in Zhu Xi's commentary and combined it with the following passage from Plutarch (again in Holland's translation):

> An honest man taketh no lesse joy and comfort in his friends, than a
> lewd person in flatterers. . . . The onley way to distinguish them a sunder
> in this point, is to marke the drift and end of the delectiation both in
> the one and the other . . . ; the whole worke of a flatterer, and the onely
> marke that he shooteth at, is alwaies to devise, prepare and confect, as it
> were, some play or sport, some action and speech, with pleasure and to do
> pleasure . . . whereas the true friend doing alwaies that which his dutie
> requireth, many times pleaseth, and as often againe he is displeasant.[120]

In other words, the difference between enjoying oneself with true friends
and enjoying oneself with flatterers is the difference between the occasional and moderate enjoyment of proper pleasures (balanced with occasional but necessary displeasures), in the case of the former, and, in the
case of the latter, a single-minded aim to pursue nothing but pleasure at
all costs. Nothing in this passage from Plutarch suggests inward or outward pleasures, which are formed entirely out of Chinese lexicography
and which lend it the exquisite aphoristic and allusive quality of classical
Chinese.

Ricci's fusion of Plutarch and Zhu Xi is nothing less than brilliant—
the creation of a truly transcultural textual moment that moreover im-
plies a subtle commentary on the language of the *Analects* insofar as it
inverts the values of *le* 樂 and *yue* 悅, in which the "joy" or "outward
pleasure" (*le* 樂) of having a true friend come from afar in Confucius is
inferior to the "happiness" or "inward pleasure" (*yue* 悅) of Ricci's true
friend, which is equivalent to the first and highest pleasure of study and
practice in Confucius. Yet this maxim of Ricci's does not make the short

list of a single Chinese writer who excerpts the work in essays or collectanea. In other words, despite Ricci's attempt in this instance to move closer to a Chinese way of thinking and writing, the effort apparently never appealed to Chinese readers. (Perhaps they found it too casual a use of Confucian terms, or, on the contrary, too ordinary.)

Likewise, when Ricci cleverly plays on the etymology of the two characters for "friend" in maxim 56, Chinese readers seem not always to have been very impressed. Jiang Xuqi (fl. 1601–1631) was interested enough in this maxim that he makes it the first of thirteen he quotes from Ricci in his own essay on friendship (1616), but Jiang quotes only the maxim proper, dispensing altogether with the inventive translingual etymological play in Chinese found in the commentary, which Ricci had deftly integrated with his translated aphorism from the *Epistles* of Cassiodorus (490?–585).[121] From a transcultural perspective, Jiang omits the best part. Wang Kentang does not seem to have objected to that part, since he includes the commentary when he quotes the maxim in his collectanea, but then he changes Ricci's "Lord on High" (*shangdi* 上帝) in the maxim to a more naturalistic "heaven" (*tian* 天), thus eliminating what would have been to Ricci its most important single element, one of the only two instances in which he mentions the divine in the essay.[122]

In other words, it seems that the best of Ricci's efforts to write something uniquely blended of Chinese and European ideas were either rejected or misread by Chinese contemporaries. And this, perhaps, is the inevitable fate of such an intercultural text—to be misrecognized as familiar when the ideas are truly strange, and to be rejected as strange when the ideas are meant to be familiar—where communication, when it does happen, is as accidental as bumping into an old friend on a distant voyage, or just as surprising and as welcome as making a new one.

NOTES

1. All translations are mine unless otherwise noted. Matteo Ricci, *Opere storiche del P. Matteo Ricci*, ed. Pietro Tacchi-Venturi, 2 vols. (Macerata: Premiato Stabilimento Tipografico, Filippo Giorgetti, 1911, 1913), 2:226.

2. For full information on these early printings, see "Chronology of Editions."

3. Ricci, *Opere storiche*, 2:248.

4. Matteo Ricci, *Fonti Ricciane*, ed. Pasquale D'Elia, 3 vols. (Rome: La Libreria dello Stato, 1942–1949), 1:369–70.

5. Wang Kentang 王肯堂, ed., *Yugang zhai bizhu* 鬱剛齋筆麈, in *Beijing tushuguan guji zhenben congkan* 北京圖書館古籍珍本叢刊 [facs. of Ming ed., 1602] (Beijing: Shumu wenxian chubanshe, 1988), 64:548–50; j. 3. On Wang Kentang, see L. Carrington Goodrich and Chaoying Fang, eds., *The Dictionary of Ming Biography, 1368–1644* [hereafter *DMB*], 2 vols. (New York: Columbia University Press, 1976), 1:104; and Ricci, *Fonti Ricciane*, 2:53.

6. For complete citations of these works, see "Texts and Variants."

7. Li Zhizao 李之藻 (1565–1630), courtesy names Wocun 我存 and Zhenzhi 振之, was born in Renhe 仁和 (Hangzhou), passed the *jinshi* examination in 1598, and held a number of important posts later in life. See Nicolas Standaert, ed., *Handbook of Christianity in China: Volume*

One: 635–1800 (Leiden: Brill, 2001), 412–13; and Arthur Hummel, ed., *Eminent Chinese of the Ch'ing Period (1644–1912)* (Washington, D.C.: Government Printing Office, 1943), 452–54. Li collaborated with Ricci on five Chinese translations of works on mathematics and cosmology. See Nicolas Standaert, "The Transmission of Renaissance Culture in Seventeenth-Century China," *Renaissance Studies* 17, no. 3 (2003): 373–74.

8. The Prince of Jian'an Commandery (建安王), named Zhu Duojie 朱多㸅, is a figure about whom we know frustratingly little except that he was enfeoffed in 1573 and died in 1601. See *DMB*, 1:139. The courtesy name that Ricci uses for him, Qianzhai 乾齋, is evidently not recorded elsewhere. See D'Elia, note in Ricci, *Fonti Ricciane*, 1:365–66. Ricci observes that he has "the title of a king," but the more generic translation of "prince" here is customary and probably more accurate.

9. Andreas Eborensis [Andrea de Rèsende, Andres Rodrigues da (d'Evora) Veiga], *Sententiae et exempla ex probatissimis quibusque scriptoribus collecta et per locos communes digesta per Andream Eborensem lusitanum* (*Wise Sayings and Illustrative Anecdotes Collected Out of the Most Virtuous Writers and Digested into Commonplaces by the Portuguese Andreas Eborensis*), 5th ed. (Paris: N. Nivellium, 1590). A copy of this very edition was found in the Jesuit Zikawei (Xujiahui 徐家匯) library in Shanghai, but it may have arrived in a later shipment of books. In his justly famous introduction to Matteo Ricci, Jonathan Spence speculates that Ricci may have *memorized* the many passages in Eborensis and quoted them without a copy of the work at hand (*The Memory Palace of Matteo Ricci* [London: Faber & Faber, 1985], 141–42). Filippo Mignini observes that several clusters

of maxims are in precisely the same order as in Eborensis, which seems to confirm its actual use, but this fact may be evidence only of Ricci's associative method of memorization (Matteo Ricci, *Dell'amicizia*, ed. Filippo Mignini [Macerata: Quodlibet, 2005], 18).

10. Ricci, *Opere storiche*, 2:226.

11. Ibid., 248.

12. "L'altro fu un trattato *De Amicitia*, nel quale, fingendo che l'istesso Re domandò al Padre che sentivano in Europa della amicitia con un modo de dialogo; et [*sic*] il Padre gli rispose con tutto quanto potette raccogliere de'nostri philosophi, santi, et tutti autori vecchi e moderni. E fece un'opra che sino adesso fa stupire a tutto questo regno" (Ricci, *Fonti Ricciane*, 1:368–69).

13. Ricci may even have been prompted by the mind-boggling popularity of the *Adages*—that collection of gems from classical authors compiled and discussed by the great reformation humanist Desiderius Erasmus. The collection not only foregrounds friendship in a number of proverbs, but also bears a dedication to a friend who Erasmus claims had urged him to write it, Lord Montjoy. (Erasmus later admitted in a letter that he had written the work on his own impulse to prove to Montjoy that his friendship was still strong despite an unfortunate incident for which Erasmus may have blamed him.) See Kathy Eden, *Friends Hold All Things in Common: Tradition, Intellectual Property, and the* Adages *of Erasmus* (New Haven, Conn.: Yale University Press, 2001), 1–3. Notably, the first of Erasmus's adages appears *twice* in Ricci's essay (in maxims 29 and 95, discussed in the section "One Rich and One Poor").

14. Ricci, *Fonti Ricciane*, 1:370.

15. For a facsimile of Ricci's world map (*Kunyu wan'guo quantu* 坤輿萬國 全圖), see Matteo Ricci, *Il mappamondo cinese del p. Matteo Ricci, S.I. (terza edizione, Pechino, 1602) conservato presso la Biblioteca vaticana*, ed. Pasquale D'Elia (Vatican City: Biblioteca Apostolica Vaticana, 1938). See also Huang Shijian 黃時鑒 and Gong Yingyan 龔纓晏, *Li Madou shijie ditu yanjiu* 利瑪竇世界地圖研究 (Shanghai: Shanghai guji chu-banshe, 2004). In fact, China appears only slightly off-center in Ricci's map, in order to make room for the Americas to the "east."

16. James Rho was the first to do so, at least in his published writing in Chinese, in the 1630s. See Nathan Sivin, "Copernicus in China," *Studia Copernicana* (Warsaw) 6 (1973): 63–122.

17. David Mungello, *Curious Land: Jesuit Accommodation and the Origins of Sinology* (Stuttgart: Franz Steiner Verlag, 1985), 110. For the argument that the accommodative method was an extension of classical hermeneu-tic practices, see Howard L. Goodman and Anthony Grafton, "Ricci, the Chinese, and the Toolkits of the Textualists," *Asia Major*, 3rd ser., 11, no. 2 (1990–1991): 95–148.

18. For more on the Rites Controversy and on the Jesuits in China generally, see Mungello, *Curious Land*; Standaert, *Handbook*, especially 309–21; Paul Rule, *K'ung-tzu or Confucius? The Jesuit Interpretation of Confucian-ism* (Sydney: Allen & Unwin, 1986); Lionel M. Jensen, *Manufacturing Confucianism: Chinese Traditions and Universal Civilization* (Durham, N.C.: Duke University Press, 1997); David Mungello, ed., *The Chinese Rites Controversy: Its History and Meaning*, Monumenta Serica Mono-graph Series 33 (Nettetal: Steyler Verlag, 1994); Spence, *Memory Palace*; Liam Matthew Brockney, *Journey to the East* (Cambridge, Mass.: Har-vard University Press, 2007); and George Harold Dunne, *Generation*

of Giants: The Story of the Jesuits in China in the Last Decades of the Ming Dynasty (Notre Dame, Ind.: University of Notre Dame Press, 1962).

19. This point is eloquently made in Jonathan Spence, "Claims and Counterclaims: The Kangxi Emperor and the Europeans (1661–1722)," in Mungello, *Chinese Rites Controversy*, 19.

20. Ricci, *Dell'amicizia*, 31–32.

21. Matteo Ricci, *Jiaoyou lun* 交友論 (Beijing, 1601), 9b. It must be noted, however, that Li Zhizao's edition cuts both these descriptions of Ricci from the colophon. Feng Yingjing 憑應京 (1555–1606), courtesy name Keda 可大, passed the *jinshi* examination in 1592. A friend and admirer of Ricci, Feng also contributed prefaces to two other of Ricci's Chinese works: the *Tianzhu shiyi* and *Ershiwu yan* 二十五言 (*Twenty-five Sayings*), in 1607. See Standaert, *Handbook*, 476, 478; and *DMB*, 2:1141.

22. Matteo Ricci, *You lun* 友論, British Library Add. Ms. 8803 [hereafter BL ms.], 27b.

23. Zhao Yifeng 趙軼峰, "Shanren yu wan Ming shehui" 山人與晚明社會, *Dongbei shida xuebao (Zhexue shehui kexue ban)* 東北師大學報 (哲學社會科學版), no. 189 (2001): 8–16.

24. "今之所謂聖人者，其與今之所謂山人者一也，特有幸不幸之異耳。幸而能詩，則自稱曰山人；幸而不能詩，則辭卻山人而以聖人名。幸而能講良知，則自稱曰聖人；不幸而不能講良知，則謝卻聖人而以山人稱" (Li Zhi 李贄, quoted in ibid., 9).

25. *DMB*, 2:1138.

26. Zhu Tingce 朱廷策 (fl. 1610), "*You lun* tici" 友論題詞, in *Baoyantang biji (guang)* 寶顏堂秘笈 (廣), ed. Chen Jiru 陳繼需, in *Baibu congshu jicheng* 百部叢書集成 [facs. of Ming ed., 1615] (Beijing: Zhonghua shuju, 1965), 18:1a.

27. This latter tradition extends to the *Congshu jicheng chupian* 叢書集成初編 (Shanghai: Shangwu yinshuguan, 1936), which is based on Chen, *Baoyantang*. See "Texts and Variants."

28. Without taking note of these associations, Ricci's modern French and Italian translators render this action as a formal *leave-taking from* the prince, rather than a *retreat into* the mountains: "Having taken my leave of him" (Ayant pris congé de lui); and, "I, Matteo, withdrew myself obediently" (Io, Matteo, mi ritirai con ossequio) (Matteo Ricci, *Le Traité de l'amitié*, ed. and trans. Philippe Che and Michel Cartier [Ermenonville: Éditions Noé, 2006], 27; Ricci, *Dell'amicizia*, 65).

29. Ricci, *You lun* (BL ms., Italian text), fol. 23v.

30. Ricci, *Fonti Ricciane*, 1:338. Haun Saussy has graciously shown me an unpublished essay that teases out contemporary Chinese impressions of Ricci as a Daoist, including the allusion to Zhuangzi in Li Zhi's honorary verses to him, which will appear in a forthcoming book, *Le Papillon chinois: Lectures interculturelles du Zhuangzi le long des siècles*. As early as Ricci's residence in Zhaoqing, rumors had spread that the Jesuits were adepts at alchemy and other such Daoist magical arts, which attracted at least one prominent disciple, Qu Rukui 瞿汝夔 (1549–1611), who printed one of the early editions of the essay on friendship. See Peter M. Engelfriet, *Euclid in China: The Genesis of the First Chinese Translation of Euclid's Elements Books I–VI (Jihe yuanben; Beijing, 1607) and Its Reception up to 1723* (Leiden: Brill, 1998), 75; and Ricci, *Fonti Ricciane*, 1:240. In what I believe to be an unknown description of Ricci in the *Jianhu ji* 堅瓠集 (*Tough Gourd Collection*), by Chu Renhu 褚人穫 (fl. 1675–1695), it is reported among other things that Ricci had mastered the powerful art of the Daoist *neiguan* 內觀 breathing technique, which allowed him to

survive diseases that killed off the rest of his companions aboard ship and which made him look decades younger than his true age at his death.

31. Ricci, *Jiaoyou lun* (1601), 1a.

32. It is worth noting that, from the earlier printed texts, Ricci seems to have invented the term *taixi* 太西 (Far West) as a back-formation from the Eurocentric notion of the Far East, not knowing that the term was already in use for an area in the south of Inner Mongolia and occasionally also for parts of India, whereas a later editor of Ricci's essay (possibly Feng, in 1601) changed it to *zuixi* 最西 (Extreme West), which must have sounded better to the ear of a late Ming scholar.

33. Ricci, *You lun* (BL ms., Italian text), fol. 1r.

34. Ricci, *You lun* (BL ms., Chinese text), 1a, and *You lun* (BL ms., Italian text), fol. 1r.

35. Reginald Hyatte, *The Arts of Friendship: The Idealization of Friendship in Medieval and Early Renaissance Literature* (Leiden: Brill, 1994), 4–5.

36. Martin Huang, "Male Friendship in Ming China: An Introduction," in *Male Friendship in Ming China*, ed. Martin Huang (Leiden: Brill, 2007), 17 [published also as a special issue of *Nan nü* 9, no. 1 (2007)]. This watershed volume is essential reading on the topic, as is Susan Mann's introduction to the AHR Forum: "Gender and Manhood in Chinese History," *American Historical Review* 105, no. 5 (2000): 1599–1666.

37. Feng, in Ricci, *Jiaoyou lun* (1601), 1b.

38. Huang notes that friendship was even the topic of a civil service exam, citing an essay by Zhong Xing 鍾惺 (1574–1625) ("Male Friendship in Ming China," 17).

39. Zhu Tingdan 朱廷旦, *Guang you lun* 廣友論, 4 *juan* (preface, 1626) [photocopy of Ming ed.], Sonkeikaku Bunko, Tokyo.

40. Ricci, *Fonti Ricciane*, 2:68. Ricci's meeting with Li Zhi may have significantly bolstered the circulation of the treatise quite apart from its printing, since the latter was famously adept at the distribution of his own works. Timothy Brook notes that the censor who wrote the memorial against Li resulting in his final imprisonment "expressed concern as much over the ease with which Li's ideas were circulating among the younger generation of provincial elites as over the ideas themselves" (*The Confusions of Pleasure: Commerce and Culture in Ming China* [Berkeley: University of California Press, 1998], 117).

41. For a note on the translation of these terms, see Martin Huang, "Male Friendship and Jiangxue (Philosophical Debates) in Sixteenth-Century China," in Huang, *Male Friendship in Ming China*, 148.

42. Ibid., 155.

43. Huang, "Male Friendship in Ming China," 32.

44. Lü Miaofen [Miaw-fen Lu] 呂妙芬, *Yangming xue shiren shequn: Lishi, sixiang yu shijian* 陽明學士人社群: 歷史、思想與實踐 (Taipei: Zhongyang yanjiu yuan jindai shi yanjiu suo, 2003), esp. 297–311.

45. Jiao Hong 焦竑, "Gucheng dawen" 古城答問, in *Danyuan ji, sishijiu juan* 澹園集四十九卷, ed. Li Jianxiong 李劍雄. Lixue congshu 理學叢書 (Beijing: Zhonghua shuju, 1999), j. 48, 735.

46. Confucius, *Lunyu* 論語 (*Analects*), 12.24. See also the *Shijing* 詩經 (*Book of Odes*), in *The Chinese Classics*, ed. James Legge, 5 vols. (London: Oxford University Press, 1897), 4:318–19.

47. Zhu Xi 朱熹, *Lunyu jizhu* 論語集注, in *Sishu jizhu* 四書集註, Sibu beiyao ed. (Shanghai: Zhonghua shuju, 1920–1933; repr., Taipei, 1990), 12.24.

48. This *chengyu* is difficult to translate, not least since scholars disagree about the precise meaning of the word *fu* (which is some kind of support on two sides that may or may not be directly related to the wheels) and about whether it means here that the *fu* and the cart rely on each other or that the two *fu* of the cart rely on each other. The *chengyu* appears in the *Zuozhuan* 左傳 (*Commentaries of Zuo*), 僖公五年 (Lord Xi, fifth year).

49. Xu Shen 許慎, *Shuowen jiezi zhu* 説文解字注, ed. Duan Yucai 段玉裁 (1815; repr., Shanghai: Shanghai guji chubanshe, 1981). I translate *peng* and *you* with different English words, but it should be noted that the two parts of the formulaic repetition may not be oppositional, at least by the time Xu Shen wrote the *Shuowen*. Instead of defining the *difference* between the two words, the two parts may be reduplicative, underlining their essential similarity. Nevertheless, the original meaning of *peng* is related to a "collection" or "gathering," whereas the original meaning of *you* is related to "help"—an etymology that Ricci cleverly plays on in maxim 56. See Li Liping 李麗萍, "'Peng' yu 'you' de ciyi fazhan"「朋」與「友」的辭意發展, *Xinan Minzu daxue xuebao (renwen sheke ban)* 西南民族大學學報 (人文社科版), no. 184 (2006): 144–47.

50. Edward Ch'ien [錢新祖], *Chiao Hung and the Restructuring of Neo-Confucianism of the Late Ming* (New York: Columbia University Press, 1986), 237.

51. *DMB*, 1:513–15, which names He's school the Cuihe tang 萃合堂. See also Ronald Dimberg, *The Sage and Society: The Life and Thought of Ho Hsin-yin* (Honolulu: University of Hawaiʻi Press, 1974), 43–47; and Wm. Theodore de Bary, "Individualism and Humanitarianism in Late Ming Thought," in *Self and Society in Ming Thought*, ed. Wm. Theodore de Bary

and the Conference on Ming Thought (New York: Columbia University Press, 1970), 178–88.

52. The third piece, *Siyou* 死友 (*Friends unto Death*), is devoted to an aspect of the heroic ideal of Chinese friendship that has nothing even roughly equivalent in Ricci's essay. See Norman Kutcher, "The Fifth Relationship: Dangerous Friendships in the Confucian Context," *American Historical Review* 105, no. 5 (2000): 1620; and *DMB*, 1:597–98.

53. This story about Master Yan is told in the *Analects* 6.9. The story about Yuan Xian is told in the *Zhuangzi* 莊子 (*The Book of Zhuangzi*), chap. 28.

54. This story is told in *juan* 17 of the *Shiji* 史記 (*Records of the Grand Historian*), in "Yuan Xian zhuan" 原憲傳 (Life of Yuan Xian), among the "Zhongni dizi zhuan" 仲尼弟子傳 (Lives of the Disciples of Confucius).

55. Gongxi Hua 公西華 was another of Confucius's disciples.

56. Xitai 西泰 was Ricci's courtesy name.

57. Xu Bo 徐勃, *Xu Shi bijing* 徐氏筆精, in *Wenyuange siku quanshu* 文淵閣四庫全書 (Taipei: Taiwan Shangwu yinshuguan, 1986), 856:576–77; j. 8, 6b–8a. My punctuation.

58. Aristotle, *Nicomachean Ethics*, trans. H. Rackham, Loeb Classical Library (Cambridge, Mass.: Harvard University Press, 1934), 19:1159b, 8:9.1.

59. Albert Augustus Trever, *A History of Greek Economic Thought* (Chicago: University of Chicago Press, 1916), 125. According to Trever, there are no known fragments, but it is quoted in Plutarch's "On Love of Wealth," in *Moralia*, 7.40.

60. Modified from *The Analects of Confucius*, trans. James Legge (Oxford: Clarendon Press, 1893), 134.

61. Zhu Xi, *Lunyu jizhu*, 10.15.

62. My translation is based on Ban Gu 班固, *Po hu t'ung* 白虎通: *The Comprehensive Discussions in the White Tiger Hall*, trans. Tjan Tjoe Som [Zeng Zhusen 曾珠森], 2 vols. (Leiden: Brill, 1949), 2:54; chap. 26. In another chapter, Ban Gu writes the following of friends: "Their property they share without reckoning. They share each other's distress and sorrow, mutually giving assistance" (貨財通而不計，共憂患而相救 [2:56; chap. 29]).

63. The *xiaogong* 小功 are the rough garments worn by those mourning the passing of older family members.

64. Scholars are fond of quoting this truncated line of Wang Kentang's in isolation as 利君遺余交友論一編，有味哉 (Master Ricci gave me a copy of the *Essay on Friendship*, which is delightful), but the *zai* 哉 is not an emphatic final particle here, but a medial exclamation marker with a postpositive subject, so that the typical quotation cuts off the subject of the sentence, which properly reads: 有味哉，其言之也! (It is delightful, the way he expresses it!).

65. The *SKTY* cuts the bracketed line, which appears in the original passage quoted from Wang Kentang, *Yugang zhai*, 64:548; j. 3, 18a. The line may refer specifically to Wang's own protracted illness: "When I was suffering, it gave me comfort." The allusion to the Western Han writer Mei Cheng 枚乘 (d. 140 B.C.E.) uses precisely the same terms famously bestowed by Wang's contemporary Yuan Hongdao 袁宏道 (1568–1610) on *Jin ping mei* 金瓶梅 (*The Plum in the Golden Vase*).

66. The description appears in the "also noted" (附錄) section of *juan* 125 in Ji Yun 紀昀, ed., *Siku quanshu zongmu tiyao* 四庫全書總目提要 [typeset ed.], 4 vols. (Shanghai: Shangwu yinshuguan, 1933), 3:707, no. 2629. I use the unpunctuated appendix to Matteo Ricci, *Jiaoyou lun*, in *Siku*

quanshu cunmu congshu 四庫全書存目叢書, ed. Sun Yancheng 孫言誠 and He Wei 賀偉 (Tainan, Taiwan: Zhuangyan wenhua shiye youxian gongsi, 1995), 93:510. Note that three of the four maxims have been slightly revised for grammatical elegance, symmetry, and concision, but not following Wang Kentang. See "Textual Variants."

67. On the political anxiety over factionalism in the Qing, see David S. Nivison, "Ho-shen and His Accusers: Ideology and Political Behavior in the Eighteenth Century," in *Confucianism in Action*, ed. David S. Nivison and Arthur F. Wright (Stanford, Calif.: Stanford University Press, 1959), 209–43; and Susan Mann, "The Male Bond in Chinese History and Culture," *American Historical Review* 105, no. 5. (2000): 1608–10.

68. Nivison, "Ho-shen and His Accusers," 218–32. For an uncanny analogue, see Erasmus's adage and commentary in Margaret Mann Phillips, *The Adages of Erasmus: A Study with Translations* (Cambridge: Cambridge University Press, 1964), 312.

69. Lü, *Yangming xue shiren shequn*, 300–303.

70. Lo Yuet Keung [Lao Yueqiang 勞悅強], "My Second Self: Matteo Ricci's Friendship in China," *Monumenta Serica* 54 (2006): 239–40. See also the chapter "Gaozi jiaoyou lun" 高子交友論, in Gao Lian 高濂, *Zunsheng bajian* 遵生八箋, ed. Zhang Ruzhe 張汝棨, Wang Dachun 王大淳, and Wang Weixin 王維新 (Chengdu: Bashu shushe, 1988).

71. My translation; compare Legge, *Analects*, 2.

72. *Mengzi* 孟子 (*The Book of Mencius*), in *The Four Books*, trans. James Legge (Shanghai: Chinese Book Company, 1933), 846; 10.8.1.

73. Huang, "Male Friendship and Jiangxue," 151; full bibliographic citations for Luo, Feng, and Gu are given in 162n.52. For a discussion of Luo's comments, see Lü, *Yangming xue shiren shequn*, 304–5.

74. Lü, *Yangming xue shiren shequn*, 306.

75. Ibid.; Huang, "Male Friendship and Jiangxue," 150.

76. Feng, in Ricci, *Jiaoyou lun* (1601), 1a–1b. The preface is reprinted in Xu Zongze 徐宗澤, ed., *Ming Qing jian Yesuhuishi yizhuo tiyao* 明清間耶穌會士譯著提要 (Beijing: Zhonghua shuju, 1949), 344. The *li*, or "Chinese mile," as it is often called, is about one-third the distance of an English mile.

77. Nicolas Standaert, *Yang Tingyun, Confucian and Christian in Late Ming China: His Life and Thought* (Leiden: Brill, 1988), 158.

78. Ibid. For more on the topic, see Douglas Lancashire, "Anti-Christian Polemics in Seventeenth Century China," *Church History* 38, no. 2 (1969): 218–41.

79. Hsü Dau-lin [Xu Daolin 徐道鄰], "The Myth of the Five Human Relationships of Confucius," *Monumenta Serica* 29 (1970–1971): 27–37.

80. Nivison, "Ho-shen and His Accusers," 209–43.

81. Kutcher, "Fifth Relationship," 1615–29.

82. Joseph McDermott, "Friendship and Its Friends in the Late Ming," in *Jinshi jiazu yu zhengzhi bijiao lishi* 近世家族與政治比較歷史, ed. Institute of Modern History, Academia Sinica (Taipei: Institute of Modern History, Academia Sinica, 1992), 1:67–96, esp. 86–88.

83. Alan Bray, *The Friend* (Chicago: University of Chicago Press, 2003), 59.

84. For more reflections of a comparative nature, see Whalen Lai, "Friendship in Confucian China: Classical and Late Ming," in *Friendship East and West: Philosophical Perspectives*, ed. Oliver Leaman (Richmond: Curzon Press, 1996), 215–50.

85. Li Zhiyan 李之彥, *Donggu suojian* 東谷所見, in *Shuofu* 説郛, ed. Tao Zongyi 陶宗儀, j. 73, *SKQS* ed., 856:153.

86. Zhang Dai 張岱, *Ye hangchuan* 夜航船 (Hangzhou: Zhejiang guji chu-banshe, 1987), 217–18. Here *dao* 導 could mean actively "leading" or pas-sively "being led" (which seems to make more sense), but the point of banding together against the prince is the same in either case.

87. De Bary, "Individualism and Humanitarianism," 186, 199. This piece by de Bary is essential reading on the topic. See also Li Zhi 李贄, *Li shi Fenshu liu juan* 李氏焚書六卷, in *Siku jinhui congshukan, ji bu* 四庫禁燬叢書刊, 集部, no. 140 [facs. of Ming ed.], ed. Siku jinhui congshu kanbian zuanwei yuanhui 四庫禁燬叢書刊編纂委員會 (Beijing: Beijing chubanshe, 2000), 3:87–89; and Cai Minglun 蔡明倫, "Li Zhi de jiao-you guan" 李贄的交友觀, *Hubei shifan xueyuan xuebao* 湖北師範學院學報 23, no. 3 (2003): 61–69.

88. Huang, "Male Friendship and Jiangxue," 161.

89. See the passage from the *Donglin shuyuan zhi* 東林書院志 (*Goals of the Eastern Grove Academy*) translated in ibid., 160–61, which had been only partially translated by McDermott ("Friendship," 81–82), as well as Huang's discussion of Lü Kun 呂坤 (1538–1618) in "Male Friendship and Jiangxue," 168–69.

90. Translated in Huang, "Male Friendship and Jiangxue," 172.

91. Pasquale D'Elia first located the source in Cicero, which is not included in Eborensis's *Sententiae et exempla*; the passage there begins: "Hoc praestat amicitia propinquitati" (This is how friendship is superior to family relations) ("Il trattato sull'amicizia: Primo libro scritto in cinese da Matteo Ricci S. I. [1595]," *Studia missionalia* 7 [1953]: 438).

92. Feng, in Ricci, *Jiaoyou lun* (1601), 1a.

93. Chen, *Baoyantang*. See also McDermott, "Friendship," 77; and Huang, "Male Friendship and Jiangxue," 147.

94. The *sancai* 三才 refer to the three spheres of nature—*tian* 天 (heaven), *di* 地 (earth), and *ren* 人 (humankind)—in a phrase dating back to the *Yijing* 易經 (*Book of Changes*). The word *tu* 圖 added to this term furthermore evokes the title of a famous late Ming encyclopedia called the *Sancai tuhui* 三才圖會 (*Collection of Drawings on the Three Subjects*), which was an illustrated compendium in one hundred *juan* of information about astrology, geography, history, and human sciences. Either the text here is missing the final word of the title (*hui*, "collection"), or Chen is simply using the word *tu* (diagram) to indicate the contents of the encyclopedia, as if to say: "Ricci is an expert in all things."

95. The term *zhendan* 震旦 (sinicized) is derived from a transliteration of the Sanskrit word for China and thus reinforces the foreign origin of the religion.

96. Mingchang 銘常 is the courtesy name of Zhu Tingce, the engraver of the edition of Ricci's essay used in Chen's collection.

97. Zuili 檇李 corresponds to the modern district of Jixing 嘉興縣, in Zhejiang 浙江省.

98. Chen, *Baoyantang*, 18:1b.

99. Zhu Mu 朱穆, courtesy name Gong Shu 公叔, was a provincial governor in Hebei under Emperor Huan Di 漢桓帝 (132–168). His biography appears in *zhuan* 傳 33 of the *Hou Han shu* 後漢書 (*Book of the Later Han*). Xiaobiao 孝標 is the courtesy name of Liu Jun 劉峻.

100. Zhu Xi 朱熹, *Zhongyong zhangju* 中庸章句, in *Sishu jizhu*, 16.1.

101. Martino Martini, *Qiuyou pian* 逑友篇, in *Tianxue chuhan* 天學初函 [facs. of Ming ed., 1629], ed. Li Zhizao 李之藻, 6 vols. (Taipei: Taiwan xuesheng shuju, 1965), 3:3a.

102.	Giuliano Bertuccioli, "Two Previously Unknown Prefaces of Ricci's *Jiao-you lun* and Martini's *Qiuyou pian* by Liu Ning and Shen Guangyu," in *Western Humanistic Culture Presented to China by Jesuit Missionaries (XVII–XVIII Centuries): Proceedings of the Conference Held in Rome, October 25–27, 1993*, ed. Federico Masini (Rome: Institutum Historicum S.I., 1996), 101–18. The article also includes facsimiles of the Chinese manuscripts.

103.	Ibid., 102.

104.	Ibid., 105–6.

105.	Vincent Cronin, *Wise Man from the West* (New York: Dutton, 1955), 128.

106.	Étienne Ducornet, Ricci's modern French biographer, for example, claims that it contains ninety-seven maxims (*Matteo Ricci: Le lettré d'Occident* [Paris: Cerf, 1992], 66; see also Joseph Dehergne, *Répertoire des Jésuites de Chine de 1552 à 1800* [Rome: Institutum Historicum S.I., 1973], 53–58]). Fang Hao's posthumous edition of Ye Delu's collation incorrectly states that the treatise is reprinted in the *Shanlin jingji ji* 山林經濟籍 (1695), which is frequently repeated by others (Ye Delu 葉德祿, "Hejiaoben Jiaoyou lun" 合校本交友論, ed. Fang Hao 方豪, *Shangzhi bianyiguan guan kan* 上智編譯館館刊 3, nos. 1 and 5 [1948]: 175, 176–88).

107.	David Mungello, "A Confucian Echo of Western Humanistic Culture in Seventeenth Century China," in Masini, *Western Humanistic Culture*, 288. Since publishing that paper over a decade ago, Mungello has read Ricci's essay and was generous in his criticism for this edition. Nor is the idea new. One of the copies in the Vatican Library (R.G. Oriente III. 233 [9]) contains a handwritten label, obviously dating to the seventeenth century, identifying it as "De Conversatione inter Amicos." It should also be noted that Chinese scholars make the same mistake—for example, Li Zhijun 李志軍, who calls the essay a selection of "76 maxims written in the form of a dialogue" (76句格言，以對話形式寫成) ("Shilun Ming Qing zhi ji Jidujiao pingdeng guannian zai Zhongguo de yingxiang" 試論明清之際基督教平等觀念在中國的影響, *Tangdu xuekan* 唐都學刊 48, no. 2 [1996]: 73).

108. Nicolas Trigault's text reads: "Fingebat P. Matthaeus (quod olim Cicero fecit in *Lelio*) se ab rege interrogatum" (Matteo Ricci and Nicolas Trigault, *De Christiana expeditione apud Sinas suscepta ab Societate* [Augsburg: Christoph. Mangium, 1615], 309).

109. Matteo Ricci and Nicolas Trigault, *China in the Sixteenth Century: The Journals of Matthew Ricci: 1583–1610*, trans. Louis Gallagher, S.J. (New York: Random House, 1953), 282.

110. Matteo Ricci, *Li Madou quanji* 利瑪竇全集, trans. Luo Yu 羅漁, 4 vols. (Taipei: Guangqi wenhua shiye, 1986), 1:255.

111. Kang Zhijie 康志杰, "Lun *Lunyu* yu *Youlun* de renlun sixiang" 論《論語》與《友論》的人倫思想, *Hanshan shifan xueyuan xuebao* 韓山師範學院學報, no. 4 (2001): 49–55.

112. Lo, "My Second Self," 221–41.

113. Ibid., 277.

114. Ibid., 228.

115. Sofia Maffei, "Fonti," in Ricci, *Dell'amicizia*, 173.

116. Plutarch, [*Moralia*], *The Philosophie, Commonlie Called, the Morals Written by the Learned Philosopher Plutarch of Chaeronea*, trans. Philemon Holland (London: Arnold Hatfield, 1603), 4.21:101.

117. Ricci, *You lun* (BL ms., Italian text), fol. 29r.

118.   Zhu Xi, *Lunyu jizhu*, 1.1.

119.   Ricci, *You lun* (BL ms., Italian text), fol. 27v.

120.   Plutarch, [*Moralia*], 4.21:91. See also Maffei, "Fonti," 168.

121.   Jiang Xuqi 江旭奇, "Jiao dao" 交道, in *Zhu yi: Bu fen juan* (*wei zhi bu*) 朱
       翼: 不分卷 (委贄部), in *Siku quanshu cunmu congshu* 四庫全書存目叢書
       [facs. of Ming ed., 1616] (Jinan: Qi Lu shushe chubanshe, 1997), 206:83.
       Ricci drew this maxim from Eborensis, *Sententiae et exempla*, 65r. These
       quotations are mentioned by Wang Zhongmin 王重民 (1903–1975) in his
       handbook on rare books but are otherwise unknown in Ricci scholarship
       and were not collated by Ye (*Zhongguo shanbenshu tiyao* 中國善本書提要
       [Shanghai: Shanghai guji chubanshe, 1983], 383).

122.   "天予人以耳目手足" (Wang Kentang, *Yugang zhai*, 64:549; j. 3, 19b).

ON FRIENDSHIP

交
友
論

答 建安王（即乾齋子）友論

歐邏巴人 利瑪竇 譔

竇也。自太西航海入中華。仰　大明天子之文德。古先王之遺教。卜室嶺表。星霜亦屢易矣。今年春時。度嶺浮江。抵於金陵。觀　上國之光。沾沾自喜。以為庶幾不負此遊也。

遠覽未周。返棹至豫章。停舟南浦。縱目西山。玩奇挹秀。計此地為至人淵藪也。低回留之不能去。遂捨舟就舍。

An Essay on Friendship in Answer to Prince Jian'an (Lord Qian Zhai)

Composed by the European, Li Madou

I, Matteo, from the Far West, have sailed across the seas and entered China with respect for the learned virtue of the Son of Heaven of the Great Ming dynasty as well as for the teachings bequeathed by the ancient kings. Since the time that I elected the place of my lodging in Lingbiao, the stars and frosts have changed several times. In the spring of this year, I crossed the mountains, sailed down the river, and arrived in Jinling, where I beheld the glory of the capital of the kingdom, which filled me with happiness, and I thought that it was not in vain that I had made this voyage.

But my long journey was not yet at an end. I sailed back to Yuzhang and moored my boat at Nanpu. I cast my gaze upon West Mountain, and I was delighted by its wondrous elegance and lushness. I thought to myself that this land must be the dwelling place of sages. Wavering for a little while between returning and staying, I finally could not depart. So I gave up my boat and took up residence there.

因而赴見　建安王。苟不鄙許之以長揖。賓序設醴驩甚。　王乃移席握
手而言曰。凡有德行之君子。辱臨吾地。未嘗不請而友且敬之。太西
邦為道義之邦。願聞其論友道何如。竇退而從迹曩少所聞。輯成友道
一帙。敬陳於左。

Thus it was that I went to visit the Prince of Jian'an Commandery. I am grateful that he did not despise me, but permitted me to greet him with a deep bow. He sat me in the place of the honored guest, and there was much wine and merriment. Then, the prince came over to me, took my hands in his, and said: "Whenever there is a traveler who is a gentleman of virtue who deigns to visit my realm, I have never failed to host him and to treat him with friendship and respect. The nations of the Far West are nations of virtue and righteousness. I wish that I could hear what their discourses on the way of friendship are like." I, Matteo, thus withdrew into seclusion, and from the sayings of old that I had heard since my youth, I compiled this Way of Friendship in one volume, which I respectfully present as follows.

1

吾友非他，即我之半，乃第二我也：故當視友如己焉。

2

友之與我，雖有二身，二身之內，其心一而已。

3

相須相佑，為結友之由。

4

孝子繼父之所交友，如承受父之產業矣。

5

時當平居無事，難指友之真偽，臨難之頃，則友之情顯焉。蓋事急之
際，友之真者益近密，偽者益踈散矣。

6

有為之君子，無異仇，必有善友。
注：如無異仇以加儆，必有善友以相資。

1

My friend is not an other, but half of myself, and thus a second me—I must therefore regard my friend as myself.

2

Although a friend and I may be of two bodies, within those two bodies there is but one heart between us.

3

Mutual need and mutual support are the reasons to make friends.

4

A devoted son will keep the friends that his father has made just as he inherits his father's wealth.

5

When life is peaceful and without trouble, it is difficult to distinguish the true from the false friend. Only when difficulties arise do the true feelings of a friend reveal themselves. For in a time of crisis, true friends will draw closer, and false friends will become increasingly scarce.

6

If an honorable man with great accomplishments has no exceptional enemies, then he must have excellent friends.

COMMENTARY: If you have no exceptional enemies to admonish you, then you must have excellent friends to support you.

7

交友之先宜察，交友之後宜信。

8

雖智者亦謬計己友，多乎實矣。

注：愚人妄自侈口，友似有而還無。智者抑或謬計，友無多而實少。

9

友之饋友而望報，非饋也，與市易者等耳。

10

友與仇，如樂與鬧，皆以和否辨之耳，故友以和為本焉：以和微業長
大，以爭大業消敗。

注：樂以導和，鬧則失和；友和則如樂，仇不和則如鬧。

7

Before making friends, we should scrutinize. After making friends, we should trust.

8

Even the wise mistakenly judge their own friends—as more in number than they are.

COMMENTARY: Fools falsely boast in order to appear to have friends when they actually have none; the wise, however, are mistaken in their reckoning: their friends are not numerous, but in fact few.

9

A friend who gives a gift to another friend and expects something in return has made no gift at all, but is no different from a trader in the marketplace.

10

Friends and enemies are like music and noise, which are distinguished only by harmony or a lack thereof. Harmony is therefore the basis of friendship. With harmony, slight things grow to greatness. With discord, great things shrivel and fail.

COMMENTARY: If music is the orchestration of harmony, then noise is the lack of harmony. The harmony of friends is like music. The discord of enemies is like noise.

在患時，吾惟喜看友之面，然或患或幸，何時友無有益？憂時減憂，
欣時增欣。

仇之惡以殘仇，深於友之愛以恩友。豈不驗世之弱于善強于惡哉？

人事情莫測，友誼難憑。今日之友，後或變而成仇，今日之仇，亦或
變而為友，可不敬慎乎？

徒試之于吾幸際，其友不可恃也。
注：脉以左手驗耳，左手不幸際也。

11

In times of trouble, the only thing that makes me happy is to see the face of a friend. Since this is so, either when troubled or when rejoicing, is there any time when a friend is not a benefit? When I am distressed, a friend decreases my distress. When I am joyous, a friend increases my joy.

12

The hatred that makes us inflict injuries upon enemies is deeper than the love that makes us bestow kindnesses upon friends. Is this not evidence that the world is weak in goodness and strong in wickedness?

13

Since human affairs cannot be foretold, friendship is difficult to rely upon. Today's friend may later change into an enemy, and today's enemy may also change into a friend. So how can we not be vigilant and cautious?

14

A friend who is tried and tested only when I am in the best of situations is one who cannot be relied upon.

COMMENTARY: We use only the left hand when taking the pulse because the left hand is for situations that are not the best.

15

既死之友，吾念之無憂，蓋在時，我有之如可失。及既亡，念之如猶在焉。

16

各人不能全盡各事，故上帝命之交友，以彼此胥助，若使除其道於世者，人類必散壞也。

17

可以與竭露發予心，始為知己之友也。

18

德志相似，其友始固。
注：爻也双又耳，彼又我，我又彼。

19

正友不常順友，亦不常逆友，有理者順之，無理者逆之，故直言獨為友之責矣。

15

I think without sadness about friends who have died, for when they were alive I held them as if I could lose them. And now that they have passed away, I think about them as if they were still alive.

16

Each person cannot fully complete every task, for which reason the Lord on High commanded that there be friendship in order that we might render aid to one another. If this Way were eradicated from the world, humankind would surely disintegrate into ruin.

17

Only the person to whom one can completely divulge and express one's heart can become the truest of true friends.

18

Only when our virtues and ambitions are alike will a friendship be solid.

COMMENTARY: The old word for *friend* 友 is simply a double *another* 又. The other is another me, and I another other.

19

Proper friends do not always agree with their friends, nor do they always disagree with their friends, but rather agree with them when they are reasonable and disagree with them when they are unreasonable. Direct speech is therefore the only responsibility of friendship.

交友如醫疾,然醫者誠愛病者,必惡其病也,彼以捄病之故,傷其體,苦其口。醫者不忍病者之身,友者宜忍友之惡乎? 諫之諫之:何恤其耳之逆,何畏其額之蹙?

友之譽及仇之訕,並不可盡信焉。

友者於友,處處時時,一而已。誠無近遠內外面背異言異情也。

友人無所善我,與仇人無所害我等焉。

20

Having a friendship is like curing an illness. This is because the physician who honestly loves the sick person must certainly hate the sickness and, in order to cure that sickness, will hurt the sick person's body and embitter the sick person's mouth. The physician cannot endure the sick body of a sufferer, so why should a friend endure the vices of their friends? Admonish them! Admonish them! Why pity their recalcitrant ears? Why fear their knitted brows?

21

Praise from one's friends and insults from one's enemies can never be completely trusted.

22

Friends with friends—in all places and at all times—are always the same. Truly, near or far, in private or in public, face-to-face or behind one another's backs, there will be no difference in their speech and no difference in their feelings.

23

A friend who does me no good is like an enemy who does me no harm.

24

友者過譽之害，較仇者過訾之害，猶大焉。

注：友人譽我，我或因而自矜。仇人訾我，我或因而加謹。

25

視財勢友人者，其財勢亡即退而離焉。謂既不見其初友之所以然，則友之情遂渙矣。

26

友之定，於我之不定事試之，可見矣。

27

爾為吾之真友，則愛我以情，不愛我以物也。

24

The harm that is done by a friend's excessive praise is greater than the harm that is done by an enemy's excessive calumny.

COMMENTARY: If a friend praises me, I may become self-conceited. If an enemy slanders me, I may become more cautious.

25

Those friends who think of one's wealth and power will withdraw and disappear when that wealth and power are gone. They will say that since they no longer see the reasons for which they began the friendship, their feelings of friendship have dissolved.

26

The stability of a friendship is both tested and revealed by the instabilities of my life.

27

If you would become my true friend, then love me out of affection; do not love me for material things.

28

交友使獨知利己，不復顧益其友，是商賈之人耳，不可謂友也。

注：小人交友如放帳，惟計利幾何。

29

友之物皆與共。

30

交友之貴賤，在所交之意耳。特據德相友者，今世得幾雙乎？

31

友之所宜相宥，有限。

注：友或負罪，惟小可容。友如犯義，必大乃棄。

32

友之樂多於義，不可久友也。

28

Whoever makes friends thinking only of personal profit without also considering the benefit of a friend is nothing more than a merchant, and cannot be called a friend.

C O M M E N T A R Y : The dishonorable man makes friends like a usurer: he merely calculates how much the interest is.

29

The material goods of friends are all held in common.

30

The value of a friendship lies in the intentions of those who make it. In this day and age, how many have befriended one another strictly for their virtue?

31

The things for which friends should forgive one another have limits.

C O M M E N T A R Y : If a friend commits a fault, and it is only very small, one may countenance it. If a friend does something morally wrong, that is a serious matter, and one must discard that friend.

32

If the pleasures of a friendship exceed what is morally right, it cannot be a long-lasting friendship.

33

忍友之惡，便以他惡為己惡焉。

34

我所能為，不必望友代為之。

35

友者古之尊名，今出之以售，比之於貨，惜哉！

36

友於昆倫邇，故友相呼謂兄，而善於兄弟為友。

37

友之益世也，大乎財焉。無人愛財為財，而有愛友特為友耳。

38

今也友既沒言，而謟諛者為佞，則惟存仇人，以我聞真語矣。

39

設令我或被害於友，非但恨己害，乃滋恨其害自友發矣。

33

If we tolerate the vices of a friend, then those vices become our own vices.

34

That which I can do myself I must not expect a friend to do for me.

35

Among the ancients, *friend* was a venerated name, but today we put it up for sale and make it comparable to a commodity. What a pity!

36

Friends are closer than brothers because friends call one another "brother," whereas the best of brothers become "friends."

37

The value of friendship in the world is greater than wealth. There is no one who loves wealth for wealth's sake, but there are those who love friendship strictly for friendship's sake.

38

These days, since friends are speechless, and flatterers have become eloquent, only by keeping my enemies am I able to hear words of truth.

39

If I should happen to be injured by a friend, I do not merely regret the injury, but I regret even more that the injury came from a friend.

40

多有密友,便無密友也。

41

如我恆幸無禍,豈識友之真否哉?

42

友之道甚廣闊,雖至下品之人以盜為事,亦必似結友為黨,方能行其
事焉。

43

視友如己者,則遐者邇,弱者強,患者幸,病者愈,何必多言耶? 死
者猶生也。

44

我有二友相訟於前,我不欲為之聽判,恐一以我為仇也;我有二仇相
訟於前,我猶可為之聽判,必一以我為友也。

40

If one has many intimate friends, then one has no intimate friends.

41

If I am constantly fortunate and never suffer misfortune, how can I distinguish a true friend from one who is not?

42

The Way of Friendship is broad and vast. It includes even men of base quality who make their living as bandits. They, too, must gather into gangs in the semblance of making friends, and only then are they able to practice their trade.

43

If we regard our friends as ourselves, then those who are distant will seem near, those who are weak will seem strong, those who are in trouble will seem fortunate, and those who are sick will seem cured. What more is there to say? Even the dead will seem to be still alive.

44

If two of my friends have a dispute in my presence, I will not act as their arbitrator for fear that one of them may consider me an enemy. If two of my enemies have a dispute in my presence, I might act as their arbitrator, for certainly one of them will consider me a friend.

45

信于仇者猶不可失，況于友者哉? 信于友不足言矣。

46

友之職，至於義而止焉。

47

如友寡也，予寡有喜，亦寡有憂焉。

48

故友為美友，不可棄之也。無故以新易舊，不久即悔。

49

既友，每事可同議定，然先須議定友。

45

Since a promise made even to an enemy must not be broken, how much more so a promise made to a friend! Faithfulness to friends goes without saying.

46

The obligation of friends extends as far as virtuous conduct will allow and no further.

47

If my friends are few, then few are my joys; and few are my worries, too.

48

An old friend is a great friend, one who should not be abandoned. If, for no reason, you change old for new, you will soon regret it.

49

With friends that we already have, we can deliberate and decide upon all matters together—but first we must deliberate and decide upon our friends.

友於親，惟此長焉，親能無相愛親。友者否，蓋親無愛親，親倫猶在。除愛乎友，其友理焉存乎?

獨有友之業能起。

友友之友，仇友之仇，為厚友也。

注：吾友必仁，則知愛人知惡人，故我據之。

不扶友之急，則臨急無助者。

50

Friends surpass family members in one point only: it is possible for family members not to love one another. But it is not so with friends. If one member of a family does not love another, the relationship of kinship still remains. But unless there is love between friends, does the essential principle of friendship exist?

51

Only business enterprises undertaken with friends can succeed.

52

To be a friend to the friends of your friends and an enemy to the friends of your enemies is the basis for a profound friendship.

COMMENTARY: Since my friends must be virtuous and benevolent, they will know whom to love and whom to hate. This is why I rely upon them.

53

If you do not support a friend in a crisis, then when you fall into a crisis yourself there will be no one to help.

俗友者同而樂多於悅，別而留憂；義友者聚而悅多於樂，散而無愧。

我能防備他人，友者安防之乎? 聊疑友，即大犯友之道矣。

上帝給人雙目、雙耳、雙手、雙足，欲兩友相助，方為事有成矣。
注：友字古篆作犮，即兩手也，可有而不可無；朋字古篆作羽，即兩
習也，鳥備之方能飛。古賢者視朋友豈不如是耶?

天下無友，則無樂焉。

54

When vulgar friends meet, their outward pleasure is greater than their inward happiness; and when they part, they have a lingering sense of unease. When virtuous friends gather, their inward happiness is greater than their outward pleasure; and after they depart, there is no feeling of shame.

55

I can be on guard against other people, but how can I be on guard against my friends? Rashly doubting a friend is a great transgression against the Way of Friendship.

56

The Lord on High gave people two eyes, two ears, two hands, and two feet so that two friends could help each other. Only in this way can deeds be brought successfully to completion.

COMMENTARY: The word for *friend* 友 in the ancient seal script is written as 𠬺, which is two hands: things are possible with them, and not possible without them. The other word for *friend* 朋 in the ancient seal script is written as 羽, which is two wings: only because birds have them are they able to fly. Did not the ancient sages thus regard friendship in the same way?

57

A world without friends is a world without joy.

以詐待友，初若可以籠人，久而詐露，反為友厭薄矣。以誠待友，初
惟自盡其心，久而誠乎，益為友敬服矣。

我先貧賤而後富貴，則舊交不可棄，而新者，或以勢利相依；我先富
貴而後貧賤，則舊交不可恃，而新者，或以道義相合。友先貧賤而後
富貴，我當察其情，恐我欲親友，而友或踈我也；友先富貴而後貧
賤，我當加其敬，恐友防我踈，而我遂自處于踈也。

夫時何時乎? 順語生友，直言生怨。

58

If you treat your friends with dishonesty, at first you will seem to have fooled them, but after a time your dishonesty will be revealed, and they will become friends who dislike and despise you. If you treat your friends with sincerity, at first you will only seem to exhaust your heart, but after a time your sincerity will become trusted, and the benefit will be the respect and admiration of your friends.

59

If I am first poor and lowly and later become rich and important, I must not abandon my old friends, for the new ones may approach me only for power and profit; if I am rich and important and later become poor and lowly, then I must not rely on my old friends, for the new ones may be drawn to me because of virtue and righteousness. If my friends are first poor and lowly and later become rich and important, I must pay attention to their feelings for fear that if I wish to become close friends, they may distance themselves from me; if my friends are first rich and important and later become poor and lowly, I must increase my respect for them for fear they may prevent me from distancing myself by doing so first, and I may thus find myself distanced against my will.

60

What sort of age is this—this age of ours? Smooth words beget friendships. Direct speech begets resentment.

視其人之友如林，則知其德之盛；視其人之友落落如晨星，則知其德之薄。

君子之交友難，小人之交友易。難合者難散，易合者易散也。

平時交好，一旦臨小利害遂為仇敵，由其交之未出於正也。交既正，則利可分，害可共矣。

我榮時請而方來，患時不請而自來，夫友哉。

61

If you see that someone's friends are like a forest, then you know that this is a person of flourishing virtue; if you see that someone's friends are as sparse as morning stars, then you know that this is a person of shallow virtue.

62

The honorable man makes friends with difficulty; the petty man makes friends with ease. What comes together with difficulty comes apart with difficulty; what comes together with ease comes apart with ease.

63

If friends who are normally on good terms one day run into a small financial loss and forthwith become adversaries, then the reasons for their having become friends was not right. If a friendship is formed for the right reasons, then profits will be divided, and losses will be shared.

64

Someone who comes to see me in my hour of glory only when invited, and who comes to see me in my hour of trouble even when not invited—now, *that* is a friend.

65

世間之物，多各而無用，同而始有益也。人豈獨不如此耶？

66

良友相交之味，失之後愈可知覺矣。

67

居染塵而狎染人，近染色，難免無污穢其身矣。交友惡人，恆聽視其醜事，必習之而浼本心焉。

68

吾偶候遇賢友，雖僅一抵掌而別，未嘗少無裨補以洽吾為善之志也。

65

Most things of this world are of no use by themselves, but only begin to be beneficial when combined with others. How could people be the one exception to this?

66

The taste of a great friendship is something that one savors all the more after one has lost it.

67

If someone lives in a dye shop and is intimate with dyers, he will be near the taint of the dye, and it will be hard to avoid polluting his body. If someone makes friends with wicked people, he will constantly see and hear shameful things; he will undoubtedly grow accustomed to them; and he will defile his heart with them.

68

If, by chance, I happen to encounter a wise friend, even if we only clap hands once and part, it is never so little that it does not reinforce my will to do good.

交友之旨無他，在彼善長於我，則我效習之；我善長於彼，則我教化之。是學而即教，教而即學，兩者互資矣。如彼善不足以效習，彼不善不可以變動，何殊盡日相與遊謔，而徒費陰影乎哉？

注：無益之友乃偷時之盜，偷時之損甚於偷財，財可復積，時則否。

使或人未篤信斯道，且修德尚危，出好入醜，心戰未決，於以剖釋其疑，安培其德而捄其將墜，計莫過于交善友，吾所數聞，所數覩，漸透於膺，豁然開悟，誠若活法勸責吾於善也。嚴哉君子！嚴哉君子！時雖言語未及，怒色未加，亦有德威以沮不善之為與。

69

The aim of making friends is none other than this: if my friends have more goodness than I do, then I must learn from them and adopt their habits; if I have more goodness than they do, then I must teach them and improve them. Learning in order to teach and teaching in order to learn are mutually beneficial. If their goodness is not worthy of studying and adopting, or if their wickedness cannot be changed, why should I exhaust whole days together with indecent pastimes and vain shadows?

COMMENTARY: A friend who is of no benefit is a thief who steals time. The loss of stolen time is much greater than that of stolen money, for money can be regained, but time cannot.

70

Suppose there is a man who has no great faith in this Way, and whose cultivation of virtue is moreover still in danger, his heart still struggling and undecided over whether he will manifest goodness or enter into shamefulness. In order to lay open and resolve his doubts, to nourish his virtue and save him from an imminent fall, I believe that there is nothing better than an excellent friend, because whatever I constantly hear and constantly see gradually sinks into my breast until I suddenly understand it all at once—truly, such a friend is like a living law that reproves me with goodness. How magnificent the honorable man is! How magnificent the honorable man is! Sometimes even without the use of speech, and even without the show of indignation, his virtuous authority can prevent immoral actions.

71

爾不得用我為友，而均為嫵媚者。

72

友者相褒之禮，易施也。夫相忍，友乃難矣。然大都友之皆感稱己之譽，而忘忍己者之德。何歟？一顯我長，一顯我短故耳。

73

一人不相愛，則耦不為友。

74

臨當用之時，俄識其非友也，愍矣。

75

務來新，戒毋誼舊者。

76

友也為貧之財，為弱之力，為病之藥焉。

77

國家可無財庫，而不可無友也。

71

If you cannot rely on me as a friend, then we are both flatterers.

72

The ritual of friends' praising one another is easy to perform. Helping one another, however, is difficult for friends. Because this is true, the great majority of friends are moved by the singing of their praises, but they forget the virtuousness of those who help them. Why is this? The reason is simply that one shows my strengths, while the other shows my weaknesses.

73

If one person does not love the other, then the two cannot be friends.

74

It is a great disappointment to learn suddenly that someone is no longer a friend just as you are about to rely on that person.

75

In seeking out the new, beware not to neglect the old.

76

A friend is the riches of the poor, the strength of the weak, and the medicine of the ill.

77

A country can do without a treasury, but it cannot do without friends.

78

仇之饋不如友之棒也。

79

世無友，如天無日，如身無目矣。

80

友者既久尋之，既少得之，既難存之，或離于眼，即念之于心焉。

81

知友之益，凡出門會人，必圖致交一新友，然後回家矣。

82

諛諂友，非友，乃偷者，偷其名而僭之耳。

83

吾福祉所致友，必吾災禍避之。

78

A gift from an enemy is worth less than a beating from a friend.

79

A world without a friend is like a heaven without a sun, like a body without eyes.

80

Since friends take a long time to seek out, since we seldom find them, and since it is difficult to keep them, it follows that whenever it is difficult to see them, you must remember them in your heart.

81

If people truly understood the benefits of friendship, then surely every time they walked out the door and met others they would make an effort to make one new friend, and only then would they return home.

82

The friend who flatters is no friend, but merely a thief who steals that name and usurps it.

83

That friend whom my prosperity has attracted will most certainly be driven away by my misfortunes.

友即結成，則戒一相斷友情；情一斷，可以姑相著而難復全矣。玉器有所黏，惡于觀，易散也而寡有用耶。

醫士之意，以苦藥瘳人病；諂友之向，以甘言干人財。

不能友己，何以友人？

智者欲離浮友，且漸而違之，非速而絕之。

欲於眾人交友，則繁焉；余竟無冤仇，則足也。

84

Once a friendship is made, do not let your mutual feelings of friendliness break even once—for that feeling, once broken, can be pieced together temporarily but only with great difficulty made whole again. When jade wares have been glued back together they are unsightly, shattered easily, and of little use.

85

The intention of the doctor is to use bitter medicine to cure a person's sickness; the goal of the flattering friend is to use sweet words to seek a person's wealth.

86

If you cannot be a friend to yourself, how can you be a friend to another?

87

The wise will seek to distance themselves from frivolous friends, and will also remove themselves gradually and not break with them suddenly.

88

Trying to make friends with everyone is complicated. In the end, avoiding people's hatred is enough.

彼非友信爾，爾不得而欺之，欺之至惡之之效也。

永德，永友之美餌矣。凡物無不以時久，為人所厭，惟德彌久，彌感
人情也。德在仇人猶，可愛。況在友者歟。

歷山王 〔大西洋古總王〕 值事急，躬入大陣，時有弼臣止之曰：事
險若斯，陛下安以免身乎？ 王曰：汝免我于詐友，且顯仇也，自乃能
防之。

89

If someone who is not your friend trusts you, then you must not cheat that person, for cheating that person will have the same effect as hating that person.

90

A lasting virtue is the ideal nourishment for a lasting friendship. There is nothing that people do not eventually grow sick of over time. Only a complete virtue will fully stir our humane sensibilities even after a long period. Virtue is admired even by our enemies. How much the more so by our friends!

91

King Li-shan (an ancient imperial monarch of the Far West) took control of a critical situation by personally entering a great battle—at which moment one of his ministers stopped him, saying: "This is dangerous! How will Your Majesty be able to save himself?" The king replied: "You protect me from crafty friends and open enemies—*these*, I can defend myself against!"

歷山王亦冀交友賢士，名為善諾，先使人奉之以數萬金，善諾怫而
曰：王眂吾以茲，意吾何人耶？ 使者曰：否也，王知夫子為至廉，是
奉之耳。曰：然則當容我為廉已矣。而麾之不受。史斷之曰：王者欲
買士之友，而士者毋賣。

歷山王未得總位時，無國庫，凡獲財厚頒給與人也。有敵國王富盛，
惟事務充庫，譏之曰：足下之庫在於何處? 曰：在於友心也。

92

King Li-shan hoped to make friends with a wise scholar named Shan-nuo, and sent ahead a messenger to present him with a gift of several tens of thousands in gold. Shan-nuo angrily said: "If the king would bestow gifts like this upon me, what kind of person must he think I am?" The messenger replied: "No, Master, it is not so. The king knows you to be incorruptible. That is why he offers this." To which he answered: "If this is so, then I will also maintain the appearance of my incorruptibility." And he indicated that he would not accept it. Historians conclude the story by saying: "The king wanted to buy the friendship of the scholar, but the scholar would not sell it."

93

At a time when King Li-shan had not yet assumed his imperial position and had no state treasury, he generously gave to others all the wealth that he gained. The king of an enemy state who was extremely wealthy and who did everything in the service of filling up his own treasury mocked him, saying: "Where is your lordship's treasury?" To which he replied: "In the hearts of my friends."

昔年有善待友而豐惠之，將盡本家產也。傍人或問之曰：財物畢與
友，何留於己乎？對曰：惠友之味也。
注：別傳對曰：留惠友之冀也。意俚異而均美焉。

古有二人同行，一極富，一極貧。或曰，二人為友至密矣。寶法德
〔古者名賢〕聞之曰：既然，何一為富者，一為貧者哉。
注：言友之物皆與共也。

昔有人求其友以非義事，而不見與之，曰：苟尔不與我所求，何復用
尔友乎？彼曰：苟尔求我以非義事，何復用尔友乎？

94

Many years ago, there was a man who treated his friends very well and who was so abundantly generous that he finally depleted his family property. Those around him asked: "When your wealth and possessions have all been given to your friends, what will you have left for yourself?" To which he replied: "The savor of having been generous to my friends."

COMMENTARY: In another version of the story, he replies: "I will still have the desire to be generous to my friends." The thoughts are different but equally beautiful.

95

In ancient times, there were two men walking together, one who was extremely rich, and one who was extremely poor. Someone commented: "Those two men have become very close friends." Hearing this, Dou-fa-de (a famous sage of antiquity) retorted: "If that is indeed so, why is it that one of them is rich and the other poor?"

COMMENTARY: That is to say, the possessions of friends should all be held in common.

96

Once upon a time, there was a man who asked a friend to do something unethical, but when the friend refused, he said: "If you will not agree to do what I ask, what good are you as a friend?" To which the other replied: "If you ask me to do what is unethical, what good are *you* as a friend?"

西土之一先王，曾交友一士，而腆養之於都中，以其為智賢者。日曠弗見陳諫，即辭之曰：朕乃人也，不能無過。汝莫見之，則非智士也；見而非諫，則非賢友也。先王弗見諫過且如此，使值近時文飾過者當何如？

是的亞〔是北方國名〕俗獨多得友者，稱之謂富也。

客力所〔西國王名〕以匹夫得大國，有賢人問得國之所行大旨，答曰：惠我友，報我仇。賢曰：不如惠友而用恩俾仇為友也。

97

An ancient king of a land in the West had made friends with a scholar and feasted him sumptuously in the capital, considering him to be a wise and virtuous man. Yet as the days passed and the king received no remonstrance, he dismissed the scholar abruptly, saying: "Since I am human, it is impossible for me not to have faults. If you do not see them, then you are not a virtuous scholar. If you do see them but make no remonstrance, then you are not a virtuous friend." This ancient king acted this way for not having received remonstrance for his faults. What do you suppose he would do if he were among the people of today, who disguise their faults with adornments?

98

In Shi-di-ya (the name of a country in the north) there is a custom that one may be called wealthy only if one has many friends.

99

Ke-li-suo (the name of a king in the West) was an ordinary man who gained a great kingdom. When a wise man asked him what his ultimate aim was in striving to gain a kingdom, he replied: "To bestow favors upon my friends, and to take revenge on my enemies." The wise man said: "It would be better to bestow favors upon your friends and to use your enemies with kindness so as to turn them into friends."

墨臥皮〔古聞士者〕折開大石榴，或人問之曰：夫子何物願獲如其子
之多耶? 曰：忠友也。

萬曆二十三年歲次乙未三月望大西洋山人/修士利瑪竇集。

When Mo-wo-pi (a renowned ancient scholar) cut open a large pome-granate, someone asked him: "Master, what things would you like to have as numerously as these seeds?" To which he responded: "Faithful friends."

COLOPHON

Compiled by Li Madou, a mountain recluse/scholar-disciple from the Far West, in the twenty-third year of the Wanli Emperor, on the ides of the third month of the *yiwei* period [1595].

CHRONOLOGY OF EDITIONS

This chronology includes only the early editions with textual authority.[1] See also "Texts and Variants."

Composition, Nanchang 南昌, 1595, winter. While living in Nanchang, Ricci composed the essay with a short introduction and seventy-six maxims.[2] He presented copies not only to the prince, Jian'an Wang 建安王, but also to many others, who were eager to transcribe it. The BL manuscript appears to represent this stage of the text.

First edition, Ningdu 甯都, 1596. The first edition (now apparently lost) was printed very soon after the essay's composition without Ricci's knowledge, probably in Ningdu (Jiangxi Province), by Su Tizhai 蘇體齋 (fl. 1590s), who was subprefect (*zhixian* 知縣) of Yingde [Yingtak] 英德, a town near Nanchang, from 1588 to 1592.[3] This edition almost certainly contained only the original seventy-six maxims.

Second edition, Nanjing 南京, 1599?. The second edition (now lost), which was printed without Ricci's approval, included a preface, dated February 1599, by Ricci's friend and later convert Qu Rukui 瞿汝夔 (1549–1611), which was reprinted in the edition of 1601 (萬曆巳亥正月殼但友人瞿汝夔序).[4] This edition probably contained only seventy-six maxims.

Third edition, Beijing 北京, 1601. The third edition is the earliest extant printed edition and the first one known for certain to contain all one hundred maxims. It was printed at the direction of Feng Yingjing 憑應京 (1555–1606), who contributed a preface. It was apparently printed without Ricci's approval, since Ricci had not yet received the necessary permission from his superiors to print the work.

Fourth edition, Beijing, 1606?. At some point, presumably after he had received permission to do so, Ricci apparently reprinted the third edition from the same blocks as those used for the 1601 edition and affixed the Jesuit seals to it.[5]

Fifth edition, Hangzhou 杭州, 1607. A fifth edition of the text was printed by Ricci's friend and collaborator Li Zhizao 李之藻 (1565–1630).

Sixth edition, Beijing, 1629. Nineteen years after Ricci's death, Li Zhizao included a slightly revised version of the text in the *Tianxue chu han* 天學初函 (*First Writings of Heavenly Studies*), along with the prefaces of Qu and Feng.

NOTES

1. This chronology is summarized from the complex debates about the uncertainties of the textual history of this work. See Joseph Dehergne and

Yan Yunliang 嚴蘊梁, "Textes et documents: Le 'Traité de l'amitié' de Matthieu Ricci," *Bulletin de l'Université de l'Aurore*, 3rd ser., 8, no. 4 (1947): 571–619; Pasquale D'Elia, "Il 'Trattato sull'amicizia': Primo libro scritto in cinese da Matteo Ricci S. I. (1595)," *Studia missionalia* 7 (1953): 425–515, and "Further Notes on Matteo Ricci's *De Amicitia*," *Monumenta Serica* 15 (1956): 356–77; and Matteo Ricci, *Dell'amicizia*, ed. Filippo Mignini (Macerata: Quodlibet, 2005), 7–34. I have also consulted the following derivative works: Fang Hao 方豪, "Li Madou *Jiaoyou lun* xin yan" 利瑪竇交友論新研, *Guoli Taiwan daxue wenshi zhexue bao* 國立臺灣大學文史哲學報 5 (1953): 137–60, and "Notes on Matteo Ricci's *De Amicitia*," *Monumenta Serica* 14 (1949–1955): 574–83; and Zou Zhenhuan 鄒振環, "Li Madou de 'Jiaoyou lun' de yikan yu chuanbo" 利瑪竇的«交友論»的譯刊與傳播, *Fudan xuebao (shehui kexue ban)* 复旦學報(社會科學版), no. 3 (2001): 49–55. As is made clear in D'Elia, "Further Notes," Fang Hao's work on the *Jiaoyou lun* was shamelessly plagiarized. See also Albert Chan, *Chinese Books and Documents in the Jesuit Archives in Rome: A Descriptive Catalogue* (Armonk, N.Y.: Sharpe, 2002), 77–79; and Louis Pfister, *Notices biographiques et bibliographiques sur les Jésuites de l'ancienne mission de Chine, 1552–1773*, 2 vols. (Shanghai: Imprimerie de la Mission Catholique, 1932, 1934), 1:35.

2. There is an apparent contradiction between Ricci's journals and the date of the text in the colophon to the 1601 edition. Ricci claims to have written the work in the winter in Nanchang, but he dates the text to *sanyue* 三月 (the third month), a time well before he had traveled to that city. D'Elia thought that it was a printer's error ("Further Notes," 356–58), but the same date appears in the BL manuscript (Matteo Ricci, *You lun*, British Library Add. Ms. 8803, 27b).

3. Su Tizhai 蘇體齋, courtesy name Dayong 大用, was a native of Ningdu 甯都. This attribution is D'Elia's very clever deduction from Ricci's journals and other research ("Further Notes," 360, 370; Matteo Ricci, *Fonti Ricciane*, ed. Pasquale D'Elia, 3 vols. [Rome: La Libreria dello Stato, 1942–1949], 1:300).

4. Qu Rukui 瞿汝夔, courtesy name Taisu 太素, was a native of Changshu 常熟, in Jiangsu Province. Baptized as Ignatius in 1605, he had met Ricci by 1592 and was one of his important advisers by 1601. See Nicolas Standaert, ed., *Handbook of Christianity in China: Volume One: 635–1800* (Leiden: Brill, 2001), 419. In a letter to Girolamo Costa, of August 15, 1599, Ricci says of the work that the Chinese have "already printed it in two places" (già la stampano in due luoghi) (*Opere storiche del P. Matteo Ricci*, ed. Pietro Tacchi-Venturi, 2 vols. [Macerata: Premiato Stabilimento Tipografico, Filippo Giorgetti, 1911–1913], 1:248). See also D'Elia, note in Ricci, *Fonti Ricciane*, 2:68.

5. An exemplar at the Biblioteca nazionale centrale in Rome (shelf mark 72.C47.1), which appears to be from this edition, is reproduced in both D'Elia, "Il 'Trattato sull'amicizia'," and Ricci, *Dell'amicizia*.

Texts and Variants

The control text for this edition is BNC, with additions from BL and *TXCH* for the title and colophon.

Manuscripts

BL   Ricci, Matteo. *You lun* 友論. British Library Add. Ms. 8803. Nanchang, ca. 1595–1599. Autograph manuscript of first draft, containing seventy-six maxims.

PUG   *Riposta del P. Matteo Ricci*. Pontificia Università Gregoriana, Ms. 292, 189–200. An anonymous Italian translation of the early seventeenth century evidently adapted from the BL manuscript. Incorrectly attributed to Ricci, it was first printed as Matteo Ricci, *Dell'amicizia*, ed. Michele Ferrucci (Pesaro, 1825; repr., Macerata, 1885), and then reproduced in Pasquale D'Elia, "Il 'Trattato sull'amicizia': Primo libro scritto in cinese da Matteo Ricci S. I. (1595)," *Studia missionalia* 7 (1953): 425–515; and Matteo Ricci, *Dell'amicizia*, ed. Filippo Mignini (Macerata: Quodlibet, 2005), 123–31.

BAV	Ricci, Matteo. *Jiaoyou lun* 交友論. Preface by Feng Ying-jing 馮應京. Beijing, 1601-1606. Vatican City: Biblioteca Apostolica Vaticana, R. G. Oriente III. 233 (9); Borg. Cin. 324 (10); Borg. Cin. 512 (4). These editions are not identical in paper cut and binding and may represent different printings even years apart, but the text in all cases is clearly printed from the same blocks, which are also the same as those of the BNF. One or more of the editions is presumably the 1601 edition or identical to it.
BCXH	Ricci, Matteo. *You lun* 友論. In *(Guang) Baichuan xuehai* (廣)百川學海 [facs. of Ming ed., 1622], 6 vols., edited by Feng Kebin 馮可賓, 4:2237-56. Taipei: Xinxing shuju, 1970.
BNC	Ricci, Matteo. *Jiaoyou lun* 交友論. Preface by Feng Ying-jing 馮應京. Beijing, 1601-1606. Biblioteca nazionale centrale, Rome, 72.C47.1. Facsimile reprinted in Ricci, *Dell'amicizia*, 62-98. Although it is impossible to date this edition any more precisely within this time frame, it is printed from different blocks from those of the BAV and BNF editions. Feng's preface is printed in a fine running script, and the edition includes the two Jesuit stamps that were affixed to approved publications.
BNF	Ricci, Matteo. *Jiaoyou lun* 交友論. Preface by Feng Ying-jing 馮應京. Beijing, 1601-1606. Bibliothèque nationale de France, Paris, Chinois 3371. See BAV.

BYT   Ricci, Matteo. *You lun* 友論. In *Baoyantang biji (guang)* 寶顏堂秘笈 (廣), edited by Chen Jiru 陳繼儒. In *Baibu congshu jicheng* 百部叢書集成 [facs. of Ming ed., 1615], vol. 18. Beijing: Zhonghua shuju, 1965. Reprint [typeset ed.], with changes [*BYT2*], Beijing: Wenming shuju, 1922.

Che   Ricci, Matteo. *Traité de l'amitié*. Edited and translated by Philippe Che and Michel Cartier. Ermenonville: Éditions Noé, 2006.

CSJC   Ricci, Matteo. *You lun* 友論. In *Congshu jicheng chupian* 叢書集成初編, edited by Wang Yunwu 王雲五, vol. 733. Shanghai: Shangwu yinshuguan, 1936. Punctuated text, based on the *BYT*.

DYJ   Jiao Hong 焦竑. *Danyuan ji, sishijiu juan* 澹園集四十九卷, j. 48. Edited by Li Jianxiong 李劍雄. Lixue congshu 理學叢書. Beijing: Zhonghua shuju, 1999.

GYL   Zhu Tingdan 朱廷但. *Guang you lun* 廣友論 [ca. 1626], 4 *juan* [photocopy of Ming ed.]. Sonkeikaku Bunko, Tokyo.

MMQC   Ricci, Matteo. *Jiaoyou lun* 交友論. In *Mingmo Qingchu Yesuhui sixiang wenxian huibian* 明末清初耶穌會思想文獻匯編, edited by Zheng Ande 鄭安德, vol. 5. Beijing: Beijing daxue zongjiao yanjiusuo, 2000.

SF   Ricci, Matteo. *You lun* 友論. In *Shuofu xuji* 説郛續集 [ca. 1646], edited by Tao Zongyi 陶宗儀, j. 30. Also in *Shuofu sanzhong* 説郛三種. Shanghai: Shanghai guji chubanshe, 1988.

SKTY   *Siku quanshu zongmu tiyao* 四庫全書總目題要, j. 125. Beijing, 1782.

TSJC	Ricci, Matteo. *Jiaoyou lun* 交友論. In *Gujin tushu jicheng* 古今圖書集成. Beijing, 1725. "Minglun huibian" 明倫彙編 (Compilation Illuminating Social Relationships), "Jiaoyi dian" 交誼典 (Part on Social Interaction), and "Pengyou bu" 朋友部 (Section on Friendship), within the category "Zonglun" 總論 (Collected Discourses).
TXCH	Ricci, Matteo. *Jiaoyou lun* 交友論. In *Tianxue chuhan* 天學初函 [facs. of Ming ed., 1629], 6 vols., edited by Li Zhizao 李之藻, 1:299–323. Taipei: Taiwan xuesheng shuju, 1965. Also in *Beijing daxue tushuguan cang Ming ke Tianxue chuhan ben* 北京大學圖書館藏明刻天學初函本. Beijing: Beijing daxue chubanshe, 1993.
XCBJ	Ricci, Matteo. *Jiaoyou lun* 交友論 [38 excerpts]. In *Xiaochuang bieji* 小窗別紀 [ca. 1614], edited by Wu Congxian 吳從先, 5:3 ("Xiji" 西紀). In *Siku quanshu cunmu congshu*, 四庫全書存目叢書, *zibu* 子部, 253:614–15; j. 3, 56a–58b. Jinan: Qi Lu shushe chubanshe, 1997. This text cuts all commentaries, which are thus not separately listed among the variants in the following. Punctuated text with errors.
XSBJ	Xu Bo 徐勃. *Xu Shi bijing* 徐氏筆精. In *Wenyuange siku quanshu* 文淵閣四庫全書, 856:576–77; j. 8, 6b–8a. Taipei: Taiwan Shangwu yinshuguan, 1986.
Ye	Ricci, Matteo. *Jiaoyou lun* 交友論. In Ye Delu 葉德祿, "Hejiaoben Jiaoyou lun" 合校本交友論, edited by Fang Hao 方豪. *Shangzhi bianyiguan guan kan* 上智編譯館館刊 3, nos. 1 and 5 (1948): 175, 176–88. A collation based on the *TXCH*.

YGZBZ	Ricci, Matteo. *Jiaoyou lun* 交友論 [39 excerpts]. In *Yugang-zhai bizhu* 鬱岡齋筆麈 [facs. of Ming ed., 1612], edited by Wang Kentang 王肯堂. In *Beijing tushuguan guji zhenben congkan* 北京圖書館古籍珍本叢刊, 64:548–50; j. 3. Beijing: Shumu wenxian chubanshe, 1988.
ZY	Ricci, Matteo. *Jiaoyou lun* 交友論 [13 excerpts]. In Jiang Xuqi 江旭奇, *Zhuyi* 朱翼. In *Siku quanshu cunmu congshu* 四庫全書存目叢書, *zibu* 子部, 206 [facs. of Ming ed., 1616; see 委贄部，交道]. Jinan: Qi Lu shushe chubanshe, 1997.

ESTIMATED TIME LINE FOR COLLECTANEA

1602	*YGZBZ*	1626	*GYL*
1606	*DYJ*	1629	*TXCH*
1614	*XCBJ*	1646	*SF*
1615	*BYT*	1725	*TSJC*
1616	*ZY*	1782	*SKTY*
1622	*BCXH*		

SELECTIONS

In the case of texts that include excerpts, the numbers of the selected maxims are listed in the order in which they appear in the indicated work.

BL	1–13, 15, 16, 18–37, 39–59, 61, 62, 63, 65–69, 70, 95, 82, 81, 80, 96, 79, 77, 76, 98, 99, 100

YGZBZ	1, 2, 4, 6, 7, 9, 12, 13, 20, 21, 23, 24, 26, 34, 35, 40, 42, 41, 43, 44, 46, 52, 53, 56, 61, 64, 65, 69, 70, 92, 95, 81, 96, 79, 77, 76, 98, 99, 100
GYL	36, 56, 7, 40, 59, 24, 69, 9, 78, 52, 93, 96, 97, 100
XCBJ	1–5, 7, 9, 13, 16–20, 23, 24, 25, 26, 28, 34, 35, 40, 43, 44, 52, 53, 56, 60, 61, 64, 66, 67, 95, 96, 79, 76
ZY	20, 56, 61 (with added text), 76, 78, 1, 4, 6, 7, 9, 24, 59, 79
XSBJ	95, 96
DYL	1
TSJC	In addition to the full text, these excerpts are spread throughout the *za lu* 雜錄 of other sections: 4 (twice), 9, 12, 19, 20, 21, 23, 24
SKTY	90, 40, 61, 95

COMMENTARIES

The Ming editions used small characters to distinguish the commentaries from the maxims, but in this edition, the former are labeled *zhu* 注 (commentary).

TITLE AND HEADING

BL	答 / 建安王〔乾齋子〕友論引
BNC	答建安王〔即乾齋子〕友論　／　大西洋耶穌會士利瑪寶述
BAV-BNF	大西域利公友論
BYT, BCXH, SF	友論 / 大西域利瑪寶集
XCBJ	友論大西域利瑪寶

| TXCH | 交友論 / 歐邏巴人利瑪竇譔 |
| TSJC | 明西域利瑪竇友論 / 雜論交友 |

PROEM

In the sections that follow, unless a subsequent variant is noted, it should be assumed that the quoted text is the same in BL, *BYT*, *BCXH*, BNC (the control text), BAV-BNF, *TXCH*, *TSJC*, Che, Ye, and any other relevant selection listed earlier. In cases where the variants are too many or too complicated to list, the entire maxim is given, as often in the case of *YGZBZ*, whose revisions offer an excellent opportunity for a comparison of literary styles.

Not in *BYT*, *BCXH*, *SF*, *TSJC*, or any text with only excerpts. 「太西」:大西 in *BYT*; 最西 in BAV-BNF, *TXCH*. | 「至人」:住人 in BL. | 「遂捨舟就舍」:遂舍舟就舍 in BL. | 「而赴見 建安王」:因憑介紹尚謁 建安王之門 in BL. | 「賓序」:冒塵賓序 in BL. | 「太西邦」:西邦 in BAV-BNF, *TXCH*.

MAXIMS

Maxims without variants are not listed.

> [Immediately preceding the first maxim:] 利瑪竇曰 in *BYT*, *BCXH*, *SF*, *XCBJ*, *TSJC*; not in BL, BNC, BAV-BNF, *YGZBZ*, *TXCH*. *GYL* precedes most excerpts with 利山人曰.

I. *YGZBZ* reads: 吾友非他即第二我也故當視友如己焉. | *DYJ* reads: 友者乃第二我也. | In *ZY* maxim reads: 友乃第二我也.

2. *YGZBZ* reads: 我與彼二身也二身之內其心一而已夫是謂之友. | *ZY* reads: 雖有二身其心一而已.

4. *YGZBZ* reads: 孝子繼父之友如繼其產業焉. | 「如承受」: 如受 in *XCBJ*.

5. *ZY* reads: 孝子繼父友如受父產. | 「偽者益」: 偽者盡 in BL, *XCBJ*.

6. Commentary not in *YGZBZ*, *BYT*, *BCXH*, *SF*, *TSJC*, *XCBJ*. | *ZY* reads: 友仇可以加儆有友可以相資.

7. *YGZBZ* reads: 未交友之先宜察，既交之後宜信. | *ZY* reads: 交先宜察交後宜信. | 「交友之後」: 友之後 in *XCBJ*.

9. *YGZBZ* reads: 友之饋友而望報焉非饋也為市焉耳矣. | *ZY* reads: 饋友望報市易等耳.

10. 「友和」: 友相和 in *BYT*, *BCXH*.

11. 「在患時吾惟喜看」: 所患者 in BL.

12. *YGZBZ* reads: 銜恨每深于懷恩記仇常切于恩友豈不驗世之弱于善彊于惡哉.

13. *YGZBZ* reads: 人情叵測交誼難憑今日之友後或變而成仇今日之仇亦或變而為友可不懼乎可不慎乎. | 「人事情」: 人情 in *BYT*; 夫事情 in *XCBJ*. | 「莫測」: 頗莫測 in *TXCH*.

14. Maxim not in BL. | 「左手」: 又手 in *TXCH*.

15. 「無憂」: 無已 in *BYT*. | 「我有之」: 我友之 in *BYT*. | 「如可失」: 如何失 in *TXCH*.

17. Maxim not in BL. | 「始」: 如 in *BCXH*, *SF*.

18. 「叏也双又耳」 in BNC, BAV-BNF, *TXCH* (alternative characters, not textual variants): 友也雙又耳 in BL, *TSJC*; 叏也雙又耳 in *BYT*; 也双又耳 in *BCXH*.

19. 「正友」: 三友 in *BCXH*. | Mispunctuated in *XCBJ*.

20. 「醫者」(twice): 醫 in *YGZBZ*. |「友者」: 友 in *YGZBZ*. |「捄」: 救 in *TSJC*. |「苦其口」: 苦其心 in *ZY*. |「宜」: 豈 in *TSJC*. |「額」: 頟 in *TSJC*.

21. 「及」not in *YGZBZ*. |「並」: 皆 in *YGZBZ*.

22. 「內外」: 外內 in BL (scribal).

23. *YGZBZ* reads: 友人無所以善我與仇人無所以害我等耳. |「無所害 我」: 無所害 in *BYT*, *BCXH*, *SF*, *TSJC*.

24. Commentary not in *ZY*.

25. 「謂既不見」: 謂此不見 in *BCXH*, *SF*, *TSJC*. |「矣」: 也 in BL, *BYT*.

27. 「不愛我以物也」: 不愛以物也 in *BYT*, *BCXH*, *SF*.

28. Commentary not in BL, *XCBJ*.

31. 「友或負罪」: 友或有罪 in *TSJC*.

36. BL uses 昆 for 昆. |「謂」: 為 in *GYL*. | Maxims 36 and 37 are combined into one in *BCXH* and *TSJC*.

37. 「 無人愛財為財」: 無以愛財為財 in *BYT*2.

38. Maxim not in BL.

39. 「我或」: 或我 in BL (scribal). |「但」: 俱 in *TSJC*.

40. 「便」: 則 in *YGZBZ*. |「也」: 矣 in *YGZBZ*; not in *SKTY*.

41. *YGZBZ* reads: 吾幸而終身無禍患不識友之真為矣. | Maxims 41 and 42 are reversed in *YGZBZ* and *TSJC*.

42. *YGZBZ* reads: 友之道甚廣雖至不肖如盜非友不能行焉. |「亦必似結 友為黨」: 亦必以結友為黨 in *TXCH*, *BYT*2. Ye rightly lists *yi* 以 as a variant in *BYT*2 for the second instance of *si* 似, but a careful examination of that character in the Ming edition shows that it was originally engraved as *si* 似, and then modified to *yi* 以, presumably by carving the radical *ren* 亻 off the block.

43. 如己者」: 如已 in *YGZBZ*. |「患者幸」not in *YGZBZ*.

44. *YGZBZ* reads: 我有二友訟於吾前吾不欲為之聽而判之恐一以吾為仇也吾有二仇訟於吾前吾猶為之聽而判之必一以我為友也.|「我猶可為之聽判」in BL, *BYT*, BNC, BAV-BNF: 我可猶為之聽判 in *TXCH*; 我猶可為之[＿]判 in *BCXH*, *SF* (blank space); 我猶可為之判 in *TSJC*.

45. Maxims 45 and 46 are combined into one in Ye.

48. 「故友」: 舊友 in BL.

52. 「知愛人知惡人」: 知友愛人知仇惡人 in BL. | Maxim and commentary are combined with 蓋 in *GYL*.

56. *YGZBZ* reads: 天予人以耳目手足，無不兩而成身者，苟非兩友相助，事何由成乎？[注]友字古篆作[篆:]爻，即兩手也，朋字古篆作[篆:]羽，即兩習也。人兩手始能握，鳥兩羽始能飛；古賢者視朋友豈不如是.|「雙目雙耳」: 雙耳雙目 in *TSJC*.|「方為事有成矣」not in *XCBJ*.|「矣」not in *ZY*. | Commentary not in *ZY*, *GYL*.|「爻」: 爻 in *BCXH*, *TSJC*; 又又 in Che (probably due to typographic limitations).|「古賢者視」: 古賢者[忄+見] in *BCXH*, *SF*.|「即兩习也」: 即兩羽也 in *BCXH*, *SF*, *TSJC*.

57. 「焉」: 也 in BL, *BCXH*, *SF*, *TSJC*.

59. 「我先富貴」: 先富貴 in *GYL*; 我先 are small characters in *BYT*. | After「道義相合」*ZY* continues: 友先富貴而後貧賤我當加其敬友先貧賤而後富貴我當察其情.

60. Not in BL.

61. 「如晨星」not in *XCBJ*. | *ZY* adds to end of maxim: 德盛者其心和平見人皆可交德簿者其心X鄙見人皆可X人當靜夜自念我所許可者多則我德日進矣我所未滿者多則我德日減以.

63. 「交好」: 交友 in Ye.

64. *YGZBZ* reads: 吾榮時招之始方來吾患時不招而自來真友哉. | Maxim not in BL.

65. 「此」: 是 in *YGZBZ*.

67. Maxim divided into two between 矣 and 交友 in *XCBJ*. |「必習之」: 必習 in *TSJC*.

69. *YGZBZ* reads: 交友之旨無他彼有善長於我則我效之我有善長於彼則我教之是學而即教教而即學互相資矣向使彼善不足以效彼不善不足教其與群嬉以謔而虛麋駒隙者何一哉. (No commentary.) | Commentary not in BL. | No maxim, only commentary, in *GYL*. |「我善長於彼」: 我善之於彼 in BNC, *BYT*, *BCXH*, *SF*, *TSJC*.

70. *YGZBZ* reads: 有人與此信道未篤執德未固出好入醜心戰未決如欲剖其疑培其德而援其將墜計莫過於交善友蓋吾所數聞所數見漸透於膺豁然開悟如行霧露之中能免沾濡嚴哉君子嚴哉君子時雖言語未及聲色未加亦有德威以潛沮其耶心而消其戾氣矣.

73. Maxim not in BL. |「一人」: 人人 in *BYT*, *BCXH*, *SF*, *TSJC*. |「友」: 及 in *BCXH*, *SF*.

74. Maxim not in BL.

75. Maxim not in BL. |「毋」: 無 in *TSJC*.

76. 「者」 not in *YGZBZ*.

77. 「也」 not in *YGZBZ*.

78. Maxim not in BL.

79. *YGZBZ* reads: 世無友如天無日人無目矣.

81. *YGZBZ* reads: 知友之益者凡出門必獲一新友而歸而後不為徒出也. |「啚」 in BNC, BAV-BNF, *TXCH*: 圖 in *BYT*, *BCXH*, *SF*, *TSJC*; not in BL.

82. 「偷者」 not in BL.

83. Maxim not in BL. | 「祉」: 社 in *BCXH*, *SF*, *TSJC*; 趾 in Ye.

84. Maxim not in BL.

85. Maxim not in BL. | 「干人財」: 長人愬 in *BCXH*, *SF*, *TSJC*.

86. Maxim not in BL. | Maxims 85 and 86 are combined into one in Ye.

87. Maxim not in BL.

88. Maxim not in BL. | 「於」: 以 in *BYT*, *BCXH*, *SF*, *TSJC*; 與 in Ye.

90. Maxim not in BL. | *SKTY* reads: 友者過譽之害大於讐者過訾之害.

91. Maxim not in BL. | 「大西洋」 in BNC: 大西域 in BAV-BNF, *BYT*, *TXCH*; 大西城 in *BCXH*, *SF*, *TSJC*.

92. Maxim not in BL. | *YGZBZ* reads: 歷山王[太西古總域王]求友賢士善諾，而使人先以幣為金萬鎰，善諾艴然曰：此何為至我王以為何人哉？使者曰：不也，王知夫子廉故以此為夫子壽。善諾曰：然則當容我為廉已矣。而麾之不受。於是國人為之語曰：王以重賞購士為友而友，而 士弗售也. | 「冀交友」: 喜交友 in *TSJC*. | 「怫」: 怖 in *TSJC*.

93. Maxim not in BL. | 「未得」: 未德 in *TSJC*. | 「總位」: 總直 in *BYT*, *BCXH*, *SF*, *GYL*, *TSJC*. | 「給與人也」: no 也 in *GYL*. | 「國王富盛」: 國[＿]富盛 (blank space) in *BCXH*, *SF*; 國富盛 in *TSJC*. | 「充」: 克 in *BCXH*, *SF*, *TSJC*.

94. Maxim not in BL. | 「與」: 於 in *TSJC*. | 「意俚異」: 意傀異 in *BCXH*, *SF*, *TSJC*; 意似異 in *BYT2*. | 「焉」 not in *BCXH*, *SF*, *TSJC*.

95. *YGZBZ* reads: 古有二人同行者一富一貧或曰此兩人者為友至密矣寶法德曰番爾何為一富而一貧哉. (No commentary.) | *XSBJ* reads: 一貧一富。號曰：相知。某人曰：既云相知，何為一貧一富哉？ | *SKTY* reads: 二人爲友，不應一富一貧. | 「或曰二人」: 或曰此二人 in BL.

96. *YGZBZ* reads: 有以非義事求諸友而友弗從其人曰爾弗從我所求何復用爾友乎友曰爾以非義事求我何復用爾友乎. |「古者名賢」:古之名賢 in *XSBJ*. |「求我以非義事」:求我以非事 in *XCBJ*.

97. Maxim not in BL. |「見而非諫」:見而弗諫 in *BYT*, *GYL*. |「先王弗見諫」:先王勿見諫 in *TSJC*.

98. *YGZBZ* reads: 是的亞〔北方國名〕俗獨得友多者稱之為富也.

99. *YGZBZ* reads: 客力所〔西國王名〕以匹夫得大國有賢人問其何以得國答曰惠我友報我仇賢者曰不如惠友而用恩致仇為友也. |「旨答」are small characters in *BYT*, *BCXH*, *SF*. |「用恩俾仇」:用恩致仇 in BL.

100. *YGZBZ* reads: 墨臥皮〔古之鬪士〕折安石榴，或人問之曰:夫子何物願獲答如其子之多耶？曰:忠友也。 |「古鬪士者」:者 not in *GYL*. |「問之曰」:曰 not in *TSJC*.

COLOPHON

BL	萬曆二十三年歲次乙未三月太西國山人利瑪竇集
BNC, BAV-BNF	萬曆二十三年歲次乙未三月望大西洋修士利瑪竇集
CSJS	萬曆二十三年歲次乙未三月望大西域山人利瑪竇集
TSJC	按友論乃西域文注辭多費解！

Not in *BCXH*, *SF*, and so on.

The following notes correspond to the numbers of the maxims in the text and translation. Sources designated with "AE" refer to Andreas Eborensis, *Sententiae et exempla*, 5th ed. (Paris: N. Nivellium, 1590). Ricci drew three-quarters of his maxims from this collection, using not only the section on *amicitia* (friendship), but also the sections on *inimicitia* (enmity), *pax* (peace), and *affinitas* (relation). The first to identify these sources was Pasquale D'Elia, "Il 'Trattato sull'amicizia': Primo libro scritto in cinese da Matteo Ricci S. I. (1595)," *Studia missionalia* 7 (1953): 425–515; and Sofia Maffei has since indentified most of the remaining sources, giving them in an appendix to Matteo Ricci, *Dell'amicizia*, ed. Filippo Mignini (Macerata: Quodlibet, 2005), 147–85, including a number of analogues. I have supplied the citation as it is recorded in Eborensis in each case with the folio numbers of the 1590 edition, but it should be stressed that since Eborensis is a digest, many of the ideas therein are quoted secondhand from other authors and often slightly rephrased to stand alone as maxims. Although Eborensis was apparently Ricci's immediate source, readers interested in the full range of classical texts should consult Maffei's appendix. Those maxims marked with an asterisk (*) were added in the second stage of composition to raise the number of seventy-six maxims to a perfect hundred.

Title. Prince of Jian'an 建安王 (the Prince of Jian'an Commandery) was a distant cousin of the emperor, with an estate in Nanchang 南昌, the capital of Jiangxi 江西 Province. See the introduction.

Proem. Lingbiao 嶺表, or Lingnan 嶺南, refers to the area south of the Wuling 五嶺 Mountains, roughly equivalent to the border region between modern Guangdong 廣東 and Guangxi 廣西 and including parts of Hunan 湖南 and Jiangxi provinces. Yuzhang is the ancient name for the region containing Nanchang. Nanpu 南浦 refers to the riverside port of Nanchang on the Gan River 贛江. Jinling 金陵 is the ancient name for the southern capital, Nanjing 南京. West Mountain (Xishan 西山), near Nanchang, is a site that has traditionally been sacred to Daoism and was the location of Wanshou Gong 萬壽宮 (Palace of Longevity). Way of Friendship 友道 could also be translated as a "doctrine" or "philosophy" or even "method" of friendship, since these senses are contained in the word *dao* 道 (way), but in order to maintain the greatest play of meanings in the Chinese, I have translated the term consistently as "Way" (see maxims 16, 42, 55, 70).

1.   Augustine, *Confessions* 4.6:2 (AE, 61v); Aristotle, *Nichomachean Ethics*, 9.4 (AE, 55r). See the introduction.

2. Aristotle, in Diogenes Laertius, *Lives of the Philosophers*, 5.1:20 (AE, 55v).

3. Cicero, *De officiis*, 23.88 (AE, 64v), and *Laelius on Friendship*, 23.88.

4. Socrates, in Plutarch, "That We Ought Not to Borrow," *Moralia*, 57.831 (AE, 55r).

5. Cicero, *Laelius*, 17.64. See maxim 41.

6. Diogenes, in Plutarch, "How to Tell a Flatterer from a Friend," *Moralia*, 4.36 (AE, 55v).

7. Seneca, *Epistles*, 1.3:2 (AE, 60r). See also maxim 49.

8. Pliny the Younger, *Epistles*, 3.2:9 (AE, 60v–61r).

9. The puns work in both languages. Ricci uses a bilingual pun on *he* 和, meaning both "peace" (*heping* 和平) and "harmony" (*heyin* 和音) and the lack thereof, which is parallel with the Latin *concordia* and *discordia*. Ambrose, *De officiis*, 3.221:125 (AE, 62r).

10. Augustine, *The City of God*, 2.21 (AE, 67r).

11. Plutarch, "Flatterer," *Moralia*, 4.2 (AE, 55r).

12. Ibid., 4.20–22 (AE, 59v).

13. Valerius Maximus, *Nine Books of Memorable Deeds and Sayings*, 7.3:3 (AE, 60v); Cicero, *Laelius*, 10.33–34, 16.160.

*14. Ricci here repeats the idea from Cicero in maxim 5 but adds an original commentary drawn from the theory of pulse diagnosis in traditional Chinese medicine. The Jesuits were fascinated by the practice, and writings on it were among the first to be translated into European languages. According to the most ancient medical classic, the *Huangdi neijing* 黃帝內經 (*Yellow Emperor's Inner Classic*): "Woman's right pulse indicates disorder, her left pulse indicates order; man's left pulse indicates disorder, while his right pulse indicates order" (女子右為逆左為從；男子左為逆右為從) (*The Yellow Emperor's Classic of Internal Medicine*, trans. Ilza Veith [Berkeley: University of California Press, 2002], 154).

15. Seneca, *Epistles*, 7.63:7 (AE, 61v).

16. At the time of the composition of this text, Ricci was still using the ancient term *Shangdi* 上帝 (the Emperor Above) to express the idea of the Christian God, although he would later prefer *Tianzhu* 天主 (Lord of Heaven) as a less controversial appropriation of terms. In the BL manuscript, Ricci translates *dao* 道 as "l'amicitia." Cicero, *For Sextus Roscius of Ameria*, 38.3 (AE, 60v).

*17. The classical term *zhiji* 知己 refers to another who knows you as you know yourself and is thus used to indicate the closest sort of friend. Augustine, *Questions*, 8.3 (AE, 62r).

18. Ricci plays with the ancient form of the character *you* 㕛 (friend) by breaking it down into a double *you* 又 (again), an adverb that he then playfully (and somewhat awkwardly) uses as a verb. He cleverly adds another level of graphic wordplay using the shorthand form of *shuang* 双 (double) instead of the full form, *shuang* 雙. The etymology is not correct, but Ricci may have known that, since he plays with the *correct* etymology in maxim 56. Ricci thus etymologizes in order to express the most fundamental idea of classical friendship in the Renaissance, the *alter idem* of maxim 1. Plutarch, "Flatterer," *Moralia*, 4.5 (AE, 55r).

19. Ibid., 4.9 (AE, 55r).

20. Augustine, *Sermons*, 49.5–6 (AE, 61v).

21. Augustine, *Against the Letters of Petilianus*, 3.10:11 (AE, 63v), and *Sermons* (AE, 61v).

22. Thales, in Diogenes, *Lives*, 1.1:37 (AE, 59v).

23. Cassiodorus, *Epistles* (AE, 62v).

24. One of the most popular of the maxims among early Chinese readers, this is the first of four quoted by the editors of the *SKTY*. See the introduction. Augustine, *Epistles*, 7.3 (AE, 62v).

25. Cicero, *The Rhetoric to Herennius*, 4.17:24 (AE, 60v).

26. Cicero, *Laelius*, 17.64 (AE, 61r). See maxim 64.

27. Cicero, *On the Ends of Good and Evil*, 2.26:85 (AE, 61r).

28. Cicero, *The Nature of the Gods*, 1.44:122 (AE, 61r).

29. The term *xiaoren* 小人 indicates a petty or shallow person in classic opposition to the *junzi* 君子, a man of noble conduct. These terms are translated throughout as "dishonorable man" and "honorable man," respectively. Aristotle, *Nichomachean Ethics*, 8.9; Pythagoras, in Diogenes, *Lives*, 8.1:10; Erasmus, *Adages*.

30. Cicero, *Good and Evil*, 2.24:78 (AE, 61r), and *Laelius*, 22.84.

31. Aulus Gellius, *Attic Nights*, 1.3:8–9 (AE, 61r); Cicero, *Laelius*, 21.76.

32. Augustine, *City of God*, 2.21 (AE, 67r); Cicero, *Laelius*, 12.83.

33. Publilius Syrus, *Sententiae*, 10 (AE, 61v).

34. Ennius, in Gellius, *Attic Nights*, 2.29:19 (AE, 61v).

35. Ovid, *Letters from the Black Sea*, 2.3:9 (AE, 61v).

36. Augustine, *Against Academics*, 2 (AE, 251v); Valerius, *Deeds and Sayings*, 4.7.

37. Aristotle, *Topoi*, 8.1 (AE, 54v).

38. Plutarch, "How to Profit by One's Enemies," *Moralia*, 2.6:89 (AE, 63r).

39. Aristotle, *Poetics*, 14 (AE, 55r).

40. Aristotle, in Diogenes, *Lives*, 5 (AE, 59v).

41. Quintilian, *Declamations*, 16 (AE, 61v). See maxim 5.

42. Cicero, *Laelius*, 23.86–87 (AE, 60r–60v).

43. Ibid., 7.23 (AE, 60r).

44. Bias, in Diogenes, *Lives*, 1.5:87.

45. Ambrose, *De officiis*, 2 (AE, 53); Augustine, *Epistles*, 205.3 (AE, 325v).

46. Diogenes, in Plutarch, "On Compliancy," *Moralia*, 41.531 (AE, 55v); Cicero, *Laelius*, 17.61.

47. Martial, *Epigrams*, 12.34 (AE, 61v).

48. Cicero, *Laelius*, 19.67–68 (AE, 61r). See also maxim 75.

49. Seneca, *Epistles*, 1.3:2 (AE, 60r). See also maxim 7.

50. Cicero, *Laelius*, 5.19.

51. Quintilian, *Institutio oratoria*, 5.11.41 (AE, 60r).

52. The word *ren* 仁, which is here translated as "virtuous and benevolent," is a key term in Confucian ethics that is difficult to render succinctly. One of the *wuchang* 五常 (five constant virtues), it encompasses the sense of humaneness and goodness. Plutarch, "Flatterer," *Moralia*, 4.24.

53. Demosthenes, *Olynthiacs*, 1 (AE, 64r).

54. See the introduction. Plutarch, "Flatterer," *Moralia*, 4.11.

55. Ricci translates *dao you* 道友 as "leggi della vera amicitia." Cicero, *Roscius*, 40.116 (AE, 64v).

56. These etymologies are based on the ancient *Shuowen jiezi* 説文解字 (*An Explanation of Graphs and Analysis of Characters*) and its commentaries. See Timothy Billings, "Making Friends with the *Kangxi zidian* 康熙字典: An Introduction" (occasional paper, April 2007, https://segue1 community.middlebury.edu/index.php?&action=site&site=tbilling& section=11854&page=48886&story=150166&detail=150166). Cassiodorus, *Epistles*, 3 (AE, 65r).

57. Aristotle, *Nichomachean Ethics*, 9.9 (AE, 54v–55r).

58. The word *xin* 心 literally means "heart," but in Chinese usage it is more equivalent to "mind" as the seat of thought and imagination and is therefore sometimes rendered as "heart-and-mind" in scholarship. It is notable, however, that Ricci often uses the term to render the Latin word *anima* (soul) from his source maxims, and renders it back into *animo* (soul) in his Italian translation in the BL manuscript, as in maxims 67, 70, and 80. Plutarch, "Flatterer," *Moralia*, 4.26.

59. The syntax at the end of this maxim is particularly difficult to construe, but the sense of the translation is correct. Compare Ricci's version: "p[er]cioche ho paura che lui si tenga già per remoto e non devo io farmi remoto" (because I fear that he may already have distanced himself and I must not hold myself at a distance) (BL ms., Italian text, fol. 28v). Cicero, *Laelius*, 15.54.

*60. Terence, in Cicero, *Laelius*, 14.89.

61. Cicero, *Laelius*, 27.100.

62. Aristotle, *Nichomachean Ethics*, 8.3; Valerius, *Deeds and Sayings*, 4.7.

63. AE, 61v: attributed to Seneca the Elder, *Declamations*.

*64. Demosthenes, in Diogenes, *Lives*, 5.5:83 (AE, 55v).

65. Cyprian, *Epistles*, 40.2:1 (AE, 67r).

66. Cicero, *Cum populo gratias egit*, 1.3 (AE, 64v).

67. The diction of this maxim strongly suggests that it is Ricci's warning against male homosexuality. See the analysis in Giovanni Vitiello, "Exemplary Sodomites: Chivalry and Love in Late Ming Culture," *Nan nü* 2, no. 2 (2000): 251. Plutarch, "On the Education of Children," *Moralia*, 1.6 (AE, 64r).

68. Plutarch, "Flatterer," *Moralia*, 4.21.

69. Ricci translates *si dao* 斯道 (this Way) as "la verita." Seneca, *Epistles*, 1.7:8 (AE, 65r); Epictetus, in Johannes Stobaeus, *Loci communes sacri et profani sententiarum* (AE, 64r-64v).

70. Seneca, *Epistles*, 15.94:40 (AE, 64v).

*71. Plutarch, *Connubialibus praeceptis*, 142 (AE, 55r); Plutarch, "Flatterer," *Moralia*, 4:23.

*72. Augustine, *De diversus quaestionibus*, 71.1 (AE, 62v); Cicero, *Laelius*, 26.97–98.

*73. AE, 54v: attributed to Plutarch, "Flatterer," *Moralia*, 4.2; Aristotle, *Ethics*, 8.2.

*74. Plutarch, "Flatterer," *Moralia*, 4.2 (AE, 55r).

*75. Cicero, *Laelius*, 19.67–68 (AE, 61r). See also maxim 48.

76. Cicero, *Laelius*, 7.23.

77. Ibid.

*78. Ambrose, *De officiis*, 1.34:173 (AE, 62v).

79. Cicero, *Laelius*, 13.47 (AE, 62v).

80. Jerome, *Epistles*, 3.6:26.

81. Aelian, *Various History*, 12 (AE, 2:128r).

82. Plutarch, "Flatterer," *Moralia*, 4:12 (AE, 55r).

*83. Ibid., 4.2. See maxim 25.

*84. Plutarch, "On Brotherly Love," *Moralia*, 34.481.

*85. AE, 243r: attributed to Saint Chrysostom; Plutarch, "Flatterer," *Moralia*, 4.11.

*86. Seneca, *Epistles*, 9.9 (AE, 61v); Augustine, *Epistles*, 258.3.

*87. Cicero, *De officiis*, 1.33.120 (AE, 61r), and *Laelius*, 21.76.

*88. Seneca, *Epistles*, 2.14:7 (AE, 63v).

*89.   Cicero, *Roscius*, 40.116 (AE, 64v).

*90.   Cicero, *Laelius*, 9.29.

*91.   Ricci's Chinese name for Alexander the Great, Lishan Wang 歷山王, literally means "Ancient Mountain." Curtius, *History of Alexander the Great*, 9.6.

*92.   Ricci's Chinese name for Phocion, Shan Nuo 善諾, literally means "Excellent Answer." Plutarch, *Life of Phocion*, 18.1–2 (AE, 2:177v, 2:314v).

*93.   Plutarch, *Life of Alexander*, 15.34.

*94.   See maxim 93.

*95.   Ricci's Chinese name for Theophrastus, Doufade 竇法德, literally means "Moral Law Virtue." See the introduction and maxim 29.

96.   Publius Rutilius Rufus (AE, 2:121v). See maxim 46.

*97.   No direct source, but for the general idea, see Plutarch, "Flatterer," *Moralia*, 4.22.

98.   Ricci's Chinese name for Scythia, Shidiya 是的亞, is merely phonetic. See maxim 51.

99.   Ricci's name for King Croesus of Lydia, Kelisuo 客力所, is phonetic but also suggests a person of great power. See Stobaeus, *Loci communes sacri et profani sententiarum*.

100.   The story from Herodotus about having faithful men in number as many as the seeds in a pomegranate involves a comment made by Darius in praise of the Persian general Megabazus. Ricci may have had the latter name in mind when he invented the "renowned ancient scholar" Mowopi 墨臥皮, whose name is merely phonetic. Herodotus, *The Histories*, 4.143.1–3.

Colophon. For a discussion of two terms *shanren* 山人 (mountain recluse) and *xiushi* 修士 (scholar-disciple), see the introduction.

Index

Aelian, 164

Alexander the Great (King Li-shan, Lishan Wang), 129, 131, 165

Ambrose, Saint, 14, 20, 159, 162, 164

Analects (Confucius), 26–27, 33, 34, 35, 38, 44, 56, 61–63

Aquaviva, Claudio, 8

Aristophanes, 28

Aristotle, 20, 27, 29, 32, 42, 158, 159, 161, 163, 164

Augustine, Saint, 14, 20, 158, 159, 160, 161, 162, 164

Aulus Gellius, 161

Ban Gu, 33, 75n.62

Beijing, 1, 2, 3, 7

Bertuccioli, Giuliano, 51

Bias, 162

Billings, Timothy, 162

Bray, Alan, 43

Brook, Timothy, 72n.40

Cartier, Michel, 70n.28

Cassiodorus, 64, 161, 162

Che, Philippe, 70n.28

Chen Jiru, 3, 17, 48–50, 79nn.94,96, 145

Ch'ien, Edward, 28

Chu Renhu, 70n.30

Cicero, Marcus Tullius, 5, 20, 47, 54, 55, 57, 78n.91, 159, 160, 161, 162, 163, 164, 165

collectanea (*congshu;* Chinese anthologies), 1, 3–4, 5, 22, 54, 55, 56, 144–55

Confucius, 12, 31, 33, 35–36, 41, 42, 56, 63, 74n.55

congshu. See collectanea

Costa, Girolamo, 8, 13, 142n.4

Croesus (Kelisuo), 135, 165

Cronin, Vincent, 54

Curtius, 165

Cyprian, 163

Damo (Bodhidharma), 37

Daoism (*dao*), 15, 17–18, 70n.30, 158, 162, 164

de Bary, Wm. Theodore, 46

debating societies (*jianghui*), 23–25, 26, 29, 38, 39–41, 46

D'Elia, Pasquale, 78n.91, 141n.2, 143n.3, 157

Demosthenes, 162, 163

Diogenes, 159, 160, 161, 162, 163

Donglin movement, 46, 78n.89

Doufade. *See* Theophrastus

Du Bo, 45, 46

Ducornet, Étienne, 80n.106

Eborensis, Andreas (Andrea de Rèsende), 8, 14, 15, 27, 42, 66n.9, 78n.91, 82n.121, 157, 158, 159, 160, 161, 162, 163, 164, 165

Erasmus, Desiderius, 20, 32, 33, 67n.13, 76n.68, 161

Essay on Friendship. See *Jiaoyou lun*

Euclid, 10

Fang Hao, 80n.106

Feng Congwu, 39

Feng Kebin, 3

Feng Yingjing (Keda), 15, 17, 22, 40–41, 47–48, 69n.21, 71n.32, 140, 144

Forbidden City, 1

Francis Xavier, Saint, 1, 5

friendship: cross-cultural, 13; as dangerous, 36–37, 43; European conceptions of, 20–21; European versus Chinese conceptions of, 43–44; Ming and Qing attitudes toward, 5, 21, 22–53, 74n.52

Gallagher, Louis, 55

Gao Lian, 37

Goa (India), 6

Gongxi Hua, 31, 74n.55

Gu Dashao, 47, 52

Gu Xiancheng, 39, 46

Guangdong (province), 6, 158

Guilford, fifth Earl of (Frederick North), 14

Gujin tushu jicheng (*TSJC; The Compendium of Ancient and Modern Books and Illustrations*), 4, 55, 146, 147, 148, 149, 150, 151, 152, 153, 154, 155

He Xinyin, 29, 37, 46, 52

Herodotus, 20, 165

Holland, Philemon, 60, 62

homosexuality, 163

Hsü Dau-lin (Xu Daolin), 42

Huan Di, 79n.99

Huang, Martin, 22, 24, 39, 40, 46, 47, 71n.38, 78n.89

Huangdi neijing (*Yellow Emperor's Inner Classic*), 159

Hyatte, Reginald, 20

Jerome, Saint, 164

Jesuits: accommodations of, to China, 2, 9, 10–13, 15–17, 53; as Daoist adepts, 70n.30; mission of, in China, 1, 6; reliance of, on Chinese scholars, 12–13; and Rites Controversy, 12; unfriendly attitudes toward, 6–7, 36, 41–42; use of Buddhist and Confucian terms by, 16–17

Jian'an Wang (Zhu Duojie; Prince of Jian'an Commandery), 7–10, 15, 34, 54, 66n.8, 87, 89, 139, 158

Jiang Xuqi, 3, 64

jianghui. See debating societies

Jiangxi (province), 7, 9, 29, 139, 158

jiangxue. See philosophical debates

Jiao Hong, 25–28

Jiaoyou lun (*Essay on Friendship;* Ricci): as biography, 53–61; British Library (BL) manuscript of, 14, 15, 16–17, 18–19, 32, 60–61, 62, 69n.21, 70nn.28,30, 71n.32, 80n.107, 139, 141n.2, 143, 147, 148, 149, 150, 151, 152, 153, 154, 155; in collectanea, 3–4, 5; colophon of, 15, 17, 141n.2, 143, 155; commentaries in, 4; composition of, 2, 7–10, 15; description of, in *SKTY*, 34–37; early editions of, 2–4, 144–47; as European or Chinese work, 19–20; exclusion of, from *SKQS*, 4, 34–37; on friendship and

Jiaoyou lun (*continued*)

    other relationships, 41–53; mention of God in, 11, 64, 160; original title of, 1; Pontificia Università Gregoriana (PUG) manuscript of, 13, 14, 143; popularity of, 2–5; proem of, 7–10; on sharing wealth, 29–38; translation of, 14–19, 58–61, 158; on traveling for friendship, 38–41. *See* also Ricci, Matteo

    MAXIMS FROM: *1*, 26–28; *16*, 11; *24*, 34; *26*, 61; *27*, 61; *29*, 31–37, 67n.13; *40*, 34; *50*, 47; *54*, 62–64; *56*, 11, 64–65, 73n.49, 82n.121; *61*, 30–36; *68*, 58–59; *74*, 61; *95*, 30–37, 67n.13

Jin Boxiang, 25–26

Jin ping mei (*The Plum in the Golden Vase;* Lanling Xiaoxiao Sheng), 75n.65

Jinling. *See* Nanjing

junzi (honorable man), 37, 161

Kelisuo. *See* Croesus

Kochi (Cochin; India), 6

Kutcher, Norman, 43

Legge, James, 38

li (Chinese mile), 77n.76

Li ji (*Book of Rites*), 28

Li Madou. *See* Ricci, Matteo

Li Xitai. *See* Ricci, Matteo

Li Zhi, 16, 22, 23, 25, 29, 37, 46, 52, 70n.30, 72n.40

Li Zhijun, 80n.107

Li Zhiyan, 44

Li Zhizao (Wocun, Zhenzhi), 3, 13, 17, 65n.7, 69n.21, 140, 146

Lingbiao, 17, 87, 158

Li-shan, King. *See* Alexander the Great

Liu Jun (Xiaobiao), 49, 79n.99

Liu Ning, 52

Liu Xiang, 45

Lo Yuet Keung (Lao Yueqiang), 37

Lü Kun, 78n.89

Lü Miaofen, 24, 25, 37, 39

Luo Hongxian, 39

Luo Yu, 56

Macao, 6

Macerata (Italy), 5

Maffei, Sofia, 59, 157, 158

Martial, 162

Martini, Martino (Wei Jitai), 4, 11, 51, 52

McDermott, Joseph, 43, 78n.89

Megabazus (Mo-wo-pi), 137, 165

Mei Cheng, 35, 75n.65

Mencius, 41, 52

Mencius, 38, 39, 42

Mignini, Filippo, 14, 66n.9, 143, 157

More, Thomas, 29

Mo-wo-pi. *See* Megabazus

Mungello, David, 11, 80n.107

Nanchang, 1, 7, 8, 34, 59, 139, 141n.2, 143, 158

Nanjing, 7, 8, 22, 158

Nie Bao, 37

Ningdu, 139, 142n.3

Nivison, David, 43

North, Frederick. *See* Guilford, fifth Earl of

Ouyang Xiu, 37, 43

Ovid, 161

philosophical debates (*jiangxue*), 23, 26

Phocion (Shan Nuo), 131, 165

Plato, 28, 32

Pliny, 159

Plutarch, 20, 58, 59–60, 62–63, 74n.59, 159, 160, 161, 162, 163, 164, 165

Prince of Jian'an Commandery. *See* Jian'an Wang

Publilius Syrus, 161

Publius Rutilius Rufus, 165

pulse diagnosis, 95, 159–60

Pythagoras, 32, 161

Qu Rukui (Taisu, Ignatius), 70n.30, 140, 142n.4

Quintilian, 161, 162

Rèsende, Andrea de. *See* Eborensis, Andreas

Rho, James, 68n.16

Ricci, Matteo: biography of, 5–6; Chinese-language skills of, 6; Chinese name of, 1, 40, 74n.56; journals of, 3, 9–10, 18; *mappamondo* of, 10–11, 19, 68n.15; self-fashioning of, as Daoist *shanren,* 15–18, 70nn.28,30. See also *Jiaoyou lun*

Ruggieri, Michele, 6, 10

Sancai tuhui (*Collection of Drawings on the Three Subjects;* Wang Qi and Wang Siyi), 79n.94

Saussy, Haun, 70n.30

School of Mind (Xinxue pai), 23–25, 28, 37

Scythia (Shidiya), 135, 156

Seneca, 20, 159, 160, 162, 164

Seneca the Elder, 163

seng (priest), 16

Shakespeare, William, 1, 13

Shan Nuo. *See* Phocion

shanren (mountain recluse), 15–18, 137, 165

Shaozhou, 7

Shen Guangyu, 51

shenfu (father), 16

shengren (sage), 16

Shidiya. *See* Scythia

Shuowen jiezi (*An Explanation of Graphs and Analysis of Characters;* Xu Shen), 28, 162

Siku quanshu (*SKQS; Complete Writings of the Four Treatises*), 4, 34

Siku quanshu zongmu tiyao (*SKTY; Synopsis of the Combined Index of the Complete Writings of the Four Treatises*), 34–36, 75n.65, 145, 147, 148, 151, 154, 161

SKQS. See Siku quanshu

SKTY. See Siku quanshu zongmu tiyao

Socrates, 159

Spence, Jonathan, 66n.9

Standaert, Nicolas, 41

Stobaeus, Johannes, 164, 165

Su Tizhai (Dayong), 139, 142n.3

Taizhou school, 23, 29, 37

Tao Zongyi, 3, 145

Terence, 163

Thales, 160

Theophrastus (Doufade), 30, 32, 133, 165

Tianxue chuhan (*TXCH; First Writings of Heavenly Studies;* Li Zhizao), 3, 15, 143, 146, 147, 149, 150, 151, 152, 153, 154

Tianzhu shiyi (*The True Meaning of the Lord in Heaven;* Ricci), 5, 69n.21

tongcai (sharing of wealth), 31, 33

tongxin (common heart-and-mind), 43

Trever, Albert Augustus, 74n.59

Trigault, Nicolas, 55, 81n.108

TSJC. See Gujin tushu jicheng

TXCH. See Tianxue chuhan

Valerius Maximus, 159, 161, 163

Veith, Ilza, 160

Vitiello, Giovanni, 163

Wang Gen, 23

Wang Ji, 39

Wang Kentang, 3, 35, 64, 75nn.64–66,
147

Wang Yangming, 23–24. *See also* School
of Mind

Wang Zhongmin, 82n.121

Wanshou Gong (Palace of Longevity),
18, 158

Wei Jitai. *See* Martini, Martino

West Mountain, 17, 87, 158

Wu Congxian, 3

wuchang (five constant virtues), 33, 162

wulun (five cardinal relationships), 25,
41–53

xiaoren (dishonorable man), 161

xin (heart-and-mind, soul), 163

Xitai. *See* Ricci, Matteo

xiushi (disciple-scholar), 15, 16, 137,
165

Xu Bo, 29–32, 34, 36, 146

Xu Guangqi, 10, 13

Yanzi (Master Yan), 30–31, 74n.53

Ye Delu, 80n.106, 82n.121, 146, 149, 151,
152, 154

Yijing (*Book of Changes*), 79n.94

Yin-Yang school, 42

you (friendship), 73n.49, 160

Yuan Hongdao, 75n.65

Yuan Xian, 30–31, 74n.53

Yuet Keung Lo, 40

zalun (miscellany treatise), 55

Zengzi, 26, 62

Zhang Anmao, 51

Zhang Dai, 45

Zhaoqing, 6, 7, 70n.30

zhiji (friend), 96, 160

Zhu Duojie. *See* Jian'an Wang

Zhu Mu (Gong Shu), 49, 79n.99

Zhu Tingce (Mingchang), 17, 69, 79n.96

Zhu Tingdan, 3, 22, 43, 48, 50, 145

Zhu Xi, 26, 33, 35, 50, 62, 63

Zigong, 31

Zuozhuan (*Commentaries of Zuo*), 73n.48